T0323789

RUSSIAN ACADEMY OF SCIENCES
INSTITUTE FOR AFRICAN STUDIES

IRINA ABRAMOVA, CURT STOLL,
KONSTANTIN TKACHENKO

GERMANY IN AFRICA: RECONCILING BUSINESS AND DEVELOPMENT

**GERMANY'S TRADE AND ECONOMIC RELATIONS
WITH AFRICAN COUNTRIES
AT THE END OF THE 20th – BEGINNING OF THE 21st CENTURY**

Edited by Prof. Dr. Leonid L. Fituni

REPRINT

MEABOOKS Inc.
Lac-Beauport
Quebec, Canada

2015

*Recommended for publication by the Scientific Council
of the Institute for African Studies of the Russian Academy of Sciences*

Reviewed by
Prof. Dr. Victor V. Drozdov, Full Professor, Economic Faculty,
Moscow State University

Dr. Valery P. Morozov, Associate Professor, Chair World Economy,
Plekhanov Economic Academy, Moscow

I. Abramova, C. Stoll, K. Tkachenko. Germany in Africa: Reconciling Business and Development. Germany's Trade and Economic Relations with African Countries at the end of the 20th– beginning of 21st century. (Edited by L. Fituni).

This is the first book on German-African economic relations published in Russia in the last 25 years. It covers a whole spectrum of Germany's bi-lateral and multilateral relations with the countries of Africa, including commercial ties, money transfers, direct and portfolio investment, movement of labor resources, etc. Special attention is given to the legal framework and political context of German-African cooperation. Germany's role in implementing EU joint policy in Africa is analyzed in detail for the first time in the Russian economic literature. The book will be of interest to scholars, university students as well as business people, interested in the contemporary economic, political and social development of Africa.

ISBN 978-0-9940325-0-8

CONTENTS

INTRODUCTION

Analysis of the complex and multi-valued processes occurring in the system of world economic relations at the end of the 20th century is of great theoretical and practical interest to Russia. Economic relations between the leading industrially developed countries of the West and developing states represent one of the important sectors of this system. The experience of Germany, one of the most economically influential powers of the world, are of particular interest in this context. An exploration of its experience of economic interaction with the less-developed regions of the world appears to be topical and useful. Nevertheless, research of these processes as applied to Africa has been remarkably scarce in the last decades.

A notable increase of West-German business interest in Africa emerged already after World War II. The "German economic miracle" stimulated West-German businessmen into exploring new markets. Africa in this regard appeared to be a sufficiently attractive and promising object of economic expansion.

It was more or less during the same historical period that the majority of African countries had freed themselves from colonial oppression and started to search for ways to diversify their foreign economic relations, paying special attention to those countries which had not previously been involved in the colonial partition of the continent – e.g. Germany, the USA, the USSR. Opportunities for German companies improved still more after a large number of countries of the continent had signed conventions on preferential treatment with the Common market (during that period, the "associated membership" was concerned), a prototype of the Yaoundé and, later, Lomé conventions. Now these countries form the ACP association under the Cotonou Agreement.

The "golden" period of African-German relations lasted almost to the end of the 1980s. Following the German reunification, as a consequence of intensification of the Maastricht process, and expansion of the European Union (EU) the significance of the African continent in the system of Germany's external economic priorities has somewhat decreased. The African markets, however, still remain an essential object of economic expansion.

A turn of Germany's interests towards Africa has in a sense become a precondition for a new qualitative, still unstudied change. The former system of relations between Africa and Germany still preserved many features of Cold War relations. Thus the features which had been typical for the post-war period, continued to dominate in the economic dialogue between Germany and Africa even after the Cold War reached its end. Once free market economics had actively spread in the world economy at the end of 1980s and 1990s, this system could not exist any longer.

A sharp deterioration of the economic climate in the African region as well as the lingering economic recession in Germany after its reunification, added to the amplification of globalization processes, accompanied by the spread of neoconservative principles in the world, have exerted a decisive influence over the formation of new tendencies in the system of German-African relations. A relative as well as absolute reduction of value amounts of German-African trade, and of the inflow of German capital to the region's countries in the 1990s arose from the slackening of the old type links. Such is one of the main manifestations of qualitative changes in the system of Germany's foreign economic relations with the developing countries of Africa.

The fact that during the recent years the theme raised by the authors of the monograph has not been actively treated in the scientific economic literature confers an additional urgency to the work. While the problems of German-African relations during the post-war period and in the 1970–1980s were rather widely covered in various works of Soviet and foreign scientists, the interest in these problems faded considerably throughout the world over the following years. Hardly more than ten rather short articles on this subject, mostly in the nature of references, have appeared in Russia throughout the entire period. Largely it is due to the fact that research has focused more on Africa itself and on the difficulties and opportunities contained in the independent African economy.

Furthermore, West-European scientists have been increasingly preoccupied with the problems of the developed countries and of the would-be EU entrants. In particular, in Germany the issues of the country's internal economic development, adaptation of the domestic economy to the challenges of globalization, European integration, and extension of the FRG influence on the countries of Eastern and Central Europe, etc. have captured increased attention.

Those German scientists, who nevertheless continue to research the problems of the developing countries, are inclined to consider the elaboration of general patterns of development of the Third World Countries altogether as a priority direction of scientific research, whereas research on Africa itself plays a relatively small role. While Africa is the most backward region, the experience of its development has not been appraised as adequately representative with relation to the mechanism of development of the Third World Countries. Subjects concerning the issues of democratization, peacemaking, proper management, combating corruption as well as traditional anthropological and ethnographic research of Africa prevail among research done by German analysts.

As for Russian (Soviet) research, the relations between the developed capitalist and the developing countries have been for a long time considered through a prism of unilateral ideological directives. The predominance of negative evaluations of the German-African economic ties (see, e.g., works by J.Etinger, M.Ochkov, S.Kozitsky), exclusively seeking out the exploiter essence frequently prevented one from seeing the actual development of economic processes in their true state. The changes which occurred in the Russian society in the late 1980s, have resulted in the appearance of the opportunity and necessity to apply a deideologized approach to research for tendencies and mechanisms of functioning of the world economy integrally as well as concerning separate regions and states.

Research of the system of German-African economic interrelations is of practical significance not only to the German business, but also to Russia. Entering the African markets, especially of the member states of the ACP, Russian external economic agencies and companies inevitably come into contact with the interests and spheres of influence of German firms. The knowledge of concrete mechanisms, customs, and standards of activity of German companies in Africa can foster the amplification of activity of the Russian business in the region, and thereafter, possibly, lead to its partnership and cooperation with German capital.

The object of research for the monograph is the particularities of Germany's foreign economic relations with the developing countries of Africa in the 1990s and the beginning of the 21st century. Thus, the main focus is the analysis of new tendencies in such spheres as trade, export of private and state capital, and aid for development.

The objective of research consists in the complex economic analysis of the changes which have occurred in scales, structure, directions, and forms of Germany's foreign economic relations with the developing countries of Africa during the above-mentioned period, as well as in revealing probable prospects of development of such relations in the near future.

A series of specific tasks has been set in order to accomplish the objective of the monograph, namely:

1. to reveal to what extent the relative decrease of Germany's interest in Africa has affected its economic stand in the region;

2. to analyze the reasons of the shift of accents of Germany's interest in the sources of raw material and markets in Africa, which have entailed changes in the value and commodity structure of the German-African trade;

8

3.   to assess German economic and technical aid to Africa, considering its focus on the support of structural reorganization programs, conducted in many countries across the continent;

4.   to characterize the shifts in scales, directions and forms of activity of German private and state capital in Africa, paying special attention to the combination of the traditional and so-called "new" forms of investment activity;

5.   to define the special role of African state members of the ACP (the group of African, Caribbean and Pacific countries) in Germany's foreign economic relations;

6.   to consider the issues concerning the traffic of labor forces (and, more generally, migration) from Africa to Germany, primarily in the context of analysis of the reasons and consequences of this process for the economy of African countries and Germany respectively.

Chronological frameworks of research cover mainly the 1990s of the 20th and the first two years of 21st century. In some cases, as more thorough research for the considered phenomenon is required, earlier temporal periods have also been considered.

A systematic approach to the investigated phenomenon underlies the research. During the work, the method of comparative analysis, and critical processing of results of expert judgments by experts from a number of German, international, and African national agencies and associations, such as UNECA (United Nations Economic Commission for Africa), OECD (Organization for Economic Cooperation and Development), German departments, etc. have been widely used.

A study of classical works on international economic relations, macroeconomics, and international capital flow by R.Vernon, J.Danning, J.Keynes, C.P.Kindleberger, A.Cairncross, A.Marshall, J.S.Mill, R.Nurkse, B.Olin, A.Ragmen, P.Samuelson, A.Phillips, S.Heymer underpins the basic economic-theoretical premise of the work.

The monograph is based on the works of a number of scientists, including those from the Institute for African Studies of the Russian Academy of Sciences; the Institute of Asian and African Studies of

Moscow State University (ISAA), the Institute of World Economy and International Relations (IMEMO), the Oriental University of the Russian Academy of Sciences, several other Russian scientific institutes. In addition, the authors used materials of several international research centers of the World Bank, International Monetary Fund (IMF), Bank for International Settlements (BIS), the United Nations Conference on Trade and Development (UNCTAD), Organization for Economic Cooperation and Development (OECD), and numerous national research centers of Germany.

In his work the authors were guided by the works of well-known Russian economists, including researchers of world trade and international capital flow, most notably T.Belous, A.Bogatyrev, V.Buglay L.Fituni and others. Research by German, African and other foreign economists, among which I.Adzhai, J.Eiserman, K.I.Amaoko should be mentioned, have been used and interpreted in the work on this monograph.

Works of the outstanding Soviet and Russian Africanists and Orientalists V. Baskin, S.Bessonov, E.Bragina, A.Vasiljev, L. Geveling served as the main theoretical base of the research.

Analysis of the preceding works, devoted to various (economic, political, and cultural) links between Germany and Africa, written by both German and Russian researchers, has played a major part. Among such works one should especially mention the works by W.Wolf, W.Kühne, K.H.Lange, I.Lileyev, S.Kozitsky, E.Mandel, M.S.Ochkov, V.Rennert, and R.Tetzlaff.

Publications of German official bodies, namely of the Federal Statistical Office of Germany (Statistisches Bundesamt Deutschland), The Federal Ministry for Economic Cooperation and Development (Bundesministerium für wirtschaftliche Zusammenarbeit und Entwicklung), German Chamber of Commerce and Industry (Deutscher Industrie– und Handelskammertag), as well as publications of International agencies such as the Economic Commission for Africa (ECA), the United Nations Conference on Trade and Development (UNCTAD), the United Nations Industrial Development Organization (UNIDO), the United Nations Centre on Transnational Corporations (UNCTC), the World Bank, the International Monetary Fund (IMF), have served as the statistical and factual basis of this monograph.

The scientific novelty of the paper consists of the fact that for the first time in post-Soviet economic literature a complex analysis of the basic tendencies of development of German-African economic links has been put into effect – under the conditions of a) intensification of the globalization process, b) in the period following the reunification of Germany, c) during and after transition of the country's leadership from the Christian democrats led by H. Kohl to the social democrats headed by G. Schröder.

An approach, free from unilateral ideological influences, has allowed an investigation of the German-African relations with respect to their specific economic contents, and an analysis of some aspects of the complex mechanisms of German-African trade relations created over decades of investment and aid policies. Isolated data from German official statistics on Africa, as well as the original documentary and statistical information of a series of official bodies of Germany, in particular, German Bank for development funding (Kreditanstalt für Wiederaufbau, KfW Entwicklungsbank), German Company for Technical Cooperation (Deutsche Gesellschaft für Technische Zusammenarbeit), German investment and development company (Deutsche Investitions- und Entwicklungsgesellschaft), German Development Service (Deutscher Entwicklungsdienst), Education Development International company (EDI) have been included in such paper for the first time. Analyses have been conducted, which have allowed evaluating the place and role of the developing states of Africa within the system of Germany's global economic links.

Of no small importance in respect to the novelty of approach is the fact that the monograph is actually the first, and so far the only research for the given issue in post-Soviet Russia, conducted by a German researcher, possessing practical operational experience in the field of German-African relations. Different views and interpretations of the same realities of international economic ties between Germany and Africa, in comparison to the works of Russian scientists, are inevitable. Gaining results of such alternative approaches, in the opinion of the authors of this monograph, is of considerable utility to the Russian study of Africa and, possibly, to social aspects altogether.

The interest to the topic was increased recently by the outbreak of the first post-Cold War global economic crisis. Despite earlier hopes to the contrary, the global financial and economic crisis is having an adverse effect on many of the most vulnerable countries in Africa. "While the initial effects of the financial crisis were slow to materialise in Africa, the impact is now becoming clear. It is sweeping away firms, mines, jobs, revenues, and livelihoods; it is in short a full blown development crisis," concluded a recent report by the African Development Bank.

This crisis threatens progress made by African countries towards achieving the Millennium Development Goals – which seek to reduce extreme poverty and its various effects. Avoiding such an outcome requires close coordination and cooperation between African and donor governments, as well as other stakeholders, including civil society, private sector and academia. Less than a week after the G20 Summit in London in 2009, the European Commission was the first to act by outlining a series of actions which the EU could take now to help developing countries weather the ongoing crisis, notably by frontloading and refocusing existing aid commitments on the most vulnerable. In addition, the Commission also initiated a process of identification of the countries hardest hit by the economic slowdown, building on a comprehensive set of vulnerability indicators at macroeconomic, social and political level. This analysis shall notably help implementing a coordinated and effective EU response, tackling the countries most in need.The book seeks to enhance the perspective on development issues on the basis of knowledge excellence, innovation and the building of bridges between the research community and policy-makers.

Chapter 1. DOCTRINAL FOUNDATIONS OF GERMANY'S ECONOMIC RELATIONS WITH AFRICA

1.1. Fundamental principles of Germany's economic cooperation with Sub-Saharan Africa within the context of common European policies

The principles underlying the new system of relations of reunified Germany with Africa were already formulated in 1992, in a special report of the Federal government on the policies concerning the African states. The authors of the report emphasized: "the objective of the German policies of development is to secure elementary living conditions for people and to provide them with an opportunity to help themselves. The German aid to the development of African states is aimed at contributing to the creation of an efficient market economy and public pluralism as prerequisites for development on the basis of their own power. It shall foster regional cooperation and integration of African countries in the World Economy" [1].

Germany considers the following to be of crucial importance in its policies of cooperation with the African states:

• providing assistance on preferential terms so as to mobilize the intrinsic opportunities of the countries of the African continent;

• comprehensive use of the principles of market economy;

• support on the part of the private German and local capital, especially from the small and medium-sized businesses;

• state support of the activity of private investors in Africa;

• observance by the partners in economic cooperation of the acknowledged international legal norms, including those in the sphere of human rights [2].

The stated principles of foreign policy of the 1990s by and large continue to apply to date. The only essential addition to them is Germany's all-out support for the NEPAD initiative (New partnership for African development) based on the neo-liberal doctrine, ideas of globalization, and recognition of the leading part of the entrepreneurial initiative.

The initiative features ideas of strengthening the democracy and "good governance", combating corruption, familiarizing the continent with the information revolution and the latest technologies. Specifically, the initiative is designed to ensure the rate of growth of the African GDP at a level of 7% in the next 15 years, and thus to halve the number of Africans living below the poverty line. It also aims to provide school education coverage for all school age children; to reduce by $^2/_3$ the infant mortality rate by 2015 and to start implementing national programs of stable development by 2005. Germany has actively worked within the framework of the "G8" towards drafting a complex of efficient financial, economic, and organizational measures capable of securing the achievement of the objectives scheduled in the program. The Federal Ministry of Economic Cooperation (FMEC) participates directly in the drafting of German approaches to the NEPAD program; its state secretary, Uschi Eid, declared that in the near future Germany would participate firsthand in securing the conditions for the implementation of this initiative.

Meanwhile, Germany, as one of leading members of the European Union, forms the principles of its policies concerning the third world countries, including the African ones, within the framework of the Pan-European approach. The former chancellor of Germany, Gerhard Schröder, had repeatedly emphasized that Germany in its foreign policy was guided by a principle of pursuing the common interests of the EU member nations[3]. The new chancellor Angela Merkel stressed in her speech to the African Union in 2007, that "it is not just Germany but the European Union as a whole that has an interest in a stable, democratic and prospering Africa. The African Union is an important partner for cooperation with us, and a significant player on the international stage. There are surely many things that we can shape together".

Since Germany's trade and economic policies concerning Africa are today formulated to a critical extent, under the influence of decisions made collectively within the EU mechanisms and according to EU Guidelines, their analysis in this paper is not only justified, but also necessary for correct understanding of the reasons and developments of the German-African economic dialogue.

At the end of the 20th century, integration processes become one of the leading trends of globalization of the world economy. Being an economic and political agency with ample power and authority, and a relatively flexible decision-making system with an extended action program, the EU has since its establishment commenced the task of drawing up a single external economic policy concerning developing countries including the African states. Germany, the European country with powerful economic potential, has played an active part in the drafting of the main principles of these policies, fixed in the Yaoundé and Lomé conventions, and nowadays – in the renewed conventions under the Cotonou agreement.

Germany, as well as other EU states, considers Africa to be a zone of interests, or "special relations". The establishment of legal, trade, economic, and political basis of these relations has occurred within the economic links of Germany and Africa. For all that, Germany employs various approaches to individual countries of Tropical and North Africa.

The countries of Tropical Africa benefited from specific advantages on the basis of the Lomé conventions. Despite low competitiveness, primary goods produced in the countries of Africa entered the German and Pan-European markets. The African states could rely on partial indemnification of the losses caused by economic fluctuations, and on certain financial aid. The EU member states, in their turn, obtained the most favorable conditions for trade and investment activity under the Lomé convention.

Yet the Lomé conventions were subject to sharp criticism from African statesmen as well as economic experts. In particular, it has been remarked that granting trade preferences on a nonreciprocal basis to African countries had not produced stable growth of their export to the EU markets. Despite increased volumes of aid in the 1980s, its scale obviously did not meet the requirements of the African states, the standard of living of the population in most of them continues to decline. Yet it is necessary to remind ourselves that the EU had not aimed to foster rapid industrialization of the African countries, entertaining the opinion that the development of manufacturing industry

15

was a task primarily for private capital, while the African states were responsible themselves for creating optimum conditions to attract foreign investors. However, some EU members, above all Germany, took measures to stimulate the increase of activity of European businessmen in Africa, already in the early 1990s.

Since the second half of the 1990s Germany (within the EU) and developing Africa have sought new forms of cooperation. A number of negotiations, at various levels, took place in 1997–2002. Germany strives to establish a partnership of a new type with the African states, with a view to create additional opportunities for German investments. In their turn, the African countries expect to set up (with Germany's help) an efficient system to promote their economic and social development, reduce their external debt by its rescheduling and cancellation, and to surmount other difficulties.

A reservation is to be made at once, that the European Union, along with Germany, considers the "African" economic policy as a component of cooperation of the EU with the African, Caribbean, and Pacific countries (ACP). While drafting the main principles of these policies, the EU is guided in particular by its economic and political interests.

Thus, for example, in the late 1990s, Germany was one of initiators of making economic-aid (and in a wider sense, development of economic cooperation) to the developing countries, including the African ones, conditional upon fulfillment of some political (or "humanitarian-democratic", as the authors of the idea formulated it) demands. The issue of relations with the ACP countries involved in armed conflicts is still one of the most vital topics. In May 1998, the European Commission presented to the EU Council of Development an analytical note prepared with the help of German experts, in which the situation with granting the EU aid to the states involved in confrontations was considered, in the context of the Lomé conventions in force at that time. As the document pointed out, the primary goal of the EU was to prevent a situation in which its means be spent on military needs, instead of on development of economic and social spheres, a situation that undermined the solidarity of the ACP member nations and impaired the strategic interests of the European countries in this region[4].

According to a number of German experts[5], integration of elements of a good governance regime into the political life of the countries of Africa has to become one of the major innovations of the agreement in preparation between the EU and the countries of the region, and can largely affect the destiny of the forthcoming agreement on trade regime. This idea has been reiterated during the second conference on the level of ministers of the EU-ACP, held in July 1999. Compromise on several moot points as to mainly political aspects of the agreement was achieved at the conference. Thus, a significant breakthrough has been accomplished in the preparation of an agreement on immigrants, being one of the "contentious issues" in the system of the EU-ACP relations. The parties have agreed upon the principle of returning of illegal immigrants to the country of residence, subject to the respect for human rights and granting a special aid package to such immigrants. They also highlighted the necessity to respect the rights of illegal immigrants, "including those in Europe".

Some disagreements still persist concerning the establishment of a good governance regime implying, among other things, combating corruption. Agreeing on this requirement by and large, the ACP states refuse to connect it to a clause of the forthcoming agreement providing for the termination of aid in case of infringement of the good governance principle. Nevertheless, as a sign of their interest in solving the issue, the ACP countries developed a counter initiative by proceeding to the preparation of a special declaration on good governance, presented subsequently at the following conference in November 1999.

No consensus was reached then as to the duration of the transitional period after the expiry of the Lomé convention: the ACP countries sought for a 10-year term, whereas Germany as well as other EU member states continued to press for a 5-year period. No decisions as to alternative patterns of regional partnership, lying outside the system of general preferences (the only one still supported by the ACP nations), were made at the conference, in spite of the work conducted by Germany's representatives to that end.

Tools of aid to developing countries appeared to be one of the stumbling blocks. Germany as well as France and partly Great Britain – the states bearing the main share of the financial burden of aid to African countries – made attempts to reform essentially the existing mechanisms in pursuance of their greater efficiency, whereas the representatives of the developing countries sought not only to preserve the guaranteed financial flows to the maximum, but even to increase them. For example, representatives of the ACP countries stated their wish to preserve the appropriate mechanisms of granting aid within the Stabex and Sysmin initiatives, as proved tools of cooperation[6].

Negotiations between the EU and the ACP states, devoted to the patterns of the future cooperation, started on September 30, 1998. Outwardly, the purposes and problems of both parties coincided: expansion and intensification of cooperation, amplification of the political dialogue, adherence to respect for human rights, combating poverty, and development of the social sphere. Nevertheless, there were significant divergences as to the means of achievement of such purposes.

Germany's representative, Billy Miller, acting at the opening of negotiations on behalf of the ACP delegation, criticized the WTO rules which, in her opinion, might not be automatically applied to all the ACP states, and suggested the period of validity of trade preferences be prolonged for more than five years without observing the reciprocity principle, as it had been planned by the EU. During negotiations, attempts were made to find a mutually acceptable compromise. Four working groups were established. The central group discussed issues of political strategy of the negotiating process as well as institutional frameworks and the political aspects of the future agreement. The other three groups were preoccupied with the discussion of development problems of the private sector, support of small and medium-sized business, economic, trade, and financial cooperation.

From September untill December 1998, each group gathered monthly to discuss these issues, preparing the first, meeting on the level of ministers of the EU-ACP countries, in the beginning of February, 1999. As a consequence, the EU and ACP experts managed to bring together the parties' standpoints as to the future agreement, destined to replace the Lomé IV convention. In particular, the following issues were agreed to:

1. The objective of cooperation. The pattern of the EU-ACP partnership should meet four basic objectives – peace, security, stability and sustainable development.

2. The main principles:

– *"Property Rights" of the ACP nations to the strategic directions of partnership.* This principle, implying the guarantee of equal rights position of the ACP states in future partnerships, respect of their sovereignty and of their right to draft their own strategy of cooperation independently, has been adopted by the experts unanimously.

– *Cooperation participants*: an agreement has been achieved concerning the fundamental openness of the future partnership for representatives of civil and private sector.

– *Differentiation*: according to the EU, the priority tasks of the partnership and methods of their accomplishment should depend on the level of development and on the needs of specific ACP states. The ACP experts prefer to speak of the "positive differentiation", which would take into consideration primarily the specific needs of the least developed countries of the region.

3. Political dialogue. From the standpoint of the EU and Germany, the frameworks of the dialogue should be as flexible as possible to allow negotiations at all the levels (global, regional, sub-regional, national, at the levels of "three", of senior officials, experts, and special envoys). This approach finds understanding with the ACP experts; however, they reject any opportunity of "dictatorship", which might be incorporated into such a pattern. Migration continues to be one of the most questionable elements of political dialogue. The German party has offered, in particular, to include a special section on illegal immigrants into the future agreement. The ACP nations consider it necessary to focus on the development and implementation of an immigrant voluntary return program.

4. Institutional frameworks. Representatives of both parties – the German and the ACP – have agreed to support the currently existing institutes (the ACP Council of Ministers and the Joint Assembly), having in mind a further increase of their efficiency. The discussion about the expediency of creation of two new institutes – summit meetings and the Council of Ministers for foreign affairs of the EU-ACP nations (the offer was put forward by the representatives of the ACP countries) is to be continued.

5. Geographical frameworks of cooperation. The European party suggested drafting new acceptance criteria to the partnership system and to set up new mechanisms of cooperation. According to the EU experts, geographical frameworks of the future partnership should not be closed for those interested to join it.

6. Validity of the convention. The ACP and the EU intended to conclude a long-term (10 to 20 years) global agreement providing for the signing of five years' financial protocols and an opportunity to revise the terms and conditions of contract every five years.

7. Default clause. Both parties have expressed their intention to give preference to the dialogue, should one of the basic elements of the future cooperation prove to be inefficient in practice; however, the ACP states want to exclude the opportunity of a unilateral decision being made by the European Union. Continuation of discussion in this matter seems to be inevitable[7].

Germany participated actively in preparations for the First Meeting of Ministers for Foreign Affairs of ACP-EC, devoted to negotiations for a new agreement, to replace in 2000 the Lomé convention (the so-called Lomé IV BIS convention), held on February 8-9, 1999 in Dakar (Senegal). An important achievement of the meeting was the drafting of a concerted position regarding the good (proper) governance regime. Certain criteria of good governance have been produced at the meeting, among them openness, availability of a legal background for the mechanism of funds allocation, administrative reform, and involvement of population in legitimation of governance and of the use of public funds, implementation of procedures for budget discussion and approval, and combating corruption.

The key issue of the validity term of trade preferences remained unsettled. Germany, acting from the concerted positions with the other EU members, pressed for an introduction of temporary restrictions on the existence of trade preferences, whereas the ACP states did not share the opinion of a number of European participants that the trade preferences regime, which had been functioning in the framework of the Yaoundé and Lomé conventions for 40 years, was favorable only to them, emphasizing that owing to such regime the EU states derived benefits from large-scale deliveries of raw material to their markets.

On the whole, the meeting clearly brought to light the basic difference in approaches of the ACP nations and the EU to solving problems of future cooperation. While for the EU members, including Germany, the key elements of the future partnership model are increasing the role of civil society, private sector, and social partners, namely primarily social innovations, from the standpoint of the ACP states the fundamental goals of the partnership are combating poverty and integrating their economic systems into the world economy. Germany under these circumstances appeared less prone to compromises in most cases than all the other EU participants.

Despite a multitude of unsettled issues, the meeting participants gave it a rather high appreciation. This was mainly due to the fact that the problem at hand was not simply the renewal of the Lomé conventions and their adaptation to the changing conditions, but a real chance to create an essentially new pattern of relations between various groups of countries, to function and develop in the third millennium. The meeting's sponsors welcomed the standpoint of Germany, which had been presiding in the EU Council and had declared for the joint initiative of the World Bank and IMF, calculated to release the external debt of the ACP countries. This initiative provided for complete cancellation of the debts of those countries in the region, where the volume of external debt had posed the main obstacle to their economic development.

The EU commission published a report based on the meeting's summary, estimating the scale and the designated purpose of economic-aid granted by the EU to these countries, describing the mechanism of control over the aid distribution as well as suggesting new ways to increase the efficiency of program implementation. The report emphasized that a combination of a number of factors, among which, not in the last place, were active efforts of the nations applying for aid, necessary for receiving such assistance. In general, the concept of economic, financial and technical support of the European states for the ACP countries underwent significant changes. The former practice of granting aid to all the countries requesting it, was abandoned. Now getting European credits is conditional upon fulfillment of a number of political demands[8].

Thus, in negotiations over a cooperation agreement, aimed at replacing the Lomé conventions, the final arrangement on the terms of its signing and the formulation of a number of problems at hand was achieved in 1999. The negotiations were held in a rather tense atmosphere, for after an abortive attempt to compromise over trade problems and over the issue of good governance regime, undertaken at the second conference at the level of ministers of foreign affairs, the prospect of reaching such an agreement prior to the expiry of the validity term of the Lomé IV convention on February 29, 2000, appeared more than doubtful. After the so-called WTO "Millennium Summit" in Seattle, where the ACP states were confronted with a rigid and uncompromising standpoint of this organization concerning the preferential regime and trade privileges for the least developed countries of the region, the approach of the ACP states' representatives to future relations with the EU, which remains their major partner in the sphere of economy and foreign trade, has changed greatly. The seemingly long ago settled issue whether the norms suggested by the WTO were to be adopted, or should efforts be made to preserve the ACP-EC preferential trade system, reappeared on the agenda.

The third round of negotiations at the level of ministers of foreign affairs of the ACP and EU countries was held on December 7–8, 1999, in Brussels. Although some progress concerning the good governance regime and the trade regime was achieved at the negotiations, a number of important issues remained unresolved. In particular, the meeting failed to settle the issue of allocation of funds within the framework of the European Development Fund (EDF) for the period 2000–2007. Although the European Development Bank had declared its willingness to allocate to the EDF needs an amount considerably exceeding the similar contribution to the previous Fund, the decision of the Foreign Affairs Ministers of the EU states to submit the issue of financial assistance granted to the ACP states for further consideration to the Union's prime ministers turned out to be a disappointment for their ACP partners. Repatriation of illegal immigrants, a contentious issue for both parties, as well as some other issues, remained unsettled. In the upshot, the main objective, namely the adoption of a document replacing the Lomé conventions, still had not been accomplished. The parties therefore decided to hold an additional meeting in February 2000.

The fourth meeting at the level of ministers of foreign affairs, held in Brussels on February 2–3, 2000, became conclusive for the achievement of a reconciled ACP-EC standpoint concerning the future of the new cooperation agreement. The parties succeeded in reaching a compromise settlement of the main moot points, notably concerning the homecoming of illegal immigrants. Following the initiative of Germany's Minister for Foreign Affairs, J. Fischer, in the agreement stipulations regarding the point in question, a special emphasis was put on respect for human rights during the repatriation of illegal immigrants. The agreement also provided for an opportunity to carry on negotiations as to the conclusion of bilateral agreements (between the EU and the ACP country directly concerned) on request of one of the parties in each specific case. A compromise was also agreed on concerning the new agreement's validity terms. Instead of the 15 years initially suggested by the EU, and the 30-year-term put forward by the ACP states, a 20-year period, which comprised two stages, was set – an 8-year preparatory stage during which the regulations of preferential trade regime shall apply, and a 12-year transitional stage, during which the most developed ACP states would conclude regional cooperation agreements with the EU.

One of the most important aspects of the agreement is a flexible individual approach to partnership between the EU and the ACP states. Though the trade preferences system is to be cancelled, the individual approach shall permit preventing the discrimination of the economically least developed countries of the region. The EU shall pave the way for the conclusion of regional cooperation agreements; however, all the ACP countries shall individually and voluntarily decide whether to conclude such agreements with the EU, depending on their opportunities. For the 38 countries of the region, falling under the category of the least developed countries, this issue shall not be put forward as a matter of principle, because they, alongside with the least developed countries of the world in general, shall benefit from duty-free access to the European markets as of 2004. They shall also receive special grants from the EU, aimed at compensating the damage from cancellation of the preferential trade regime and at softening the economic and social consequences of entry into the open market system.

Taking into consideration the fact that the Lomé IV convention expired on February 29, 2000, the EU Commission put forward the following measures towards the filling of the emerging legal vacuum. These measures included, in particular:

- in the period between March 1, 2000, and May 31, 2000, postponing the implementation of the present Lomé conventions, except for its trade protocols. The application of regulations on the 8-year trade regime (2000-2008), concerning the preparation of regional economic agreements of cooperation and partnership.

- in the period between May 31, 2000, and the date on which the agreement is to come into effect, implementing the new agreement, without waiting for the completion of ratification procedures. However, some amendments concerning the direct expenditure of funds bear no legal nature pending the entry of the EDF financial protocol into force.

Thus, one can ascertain that the lengthy and intricate process of preparing an agreement to replace the Lomé conventions, which would take into account the changes determining the modern political and economic situation, came to an end. Germany's initiatives were of considerable importance to this process.

New regulations, referred to as "transitional measures", went into effect on March 1, 2000. The committee of ambassadors of the ACP-EC, having received a mandate of the joint Council of Ministers of the ACP-EC, decided to prolong the action of the Lomé IV conventions untill August 1, 2000, except for the issues regarding the trade regime. The exact limits of the second phase of the "transitional measures" are to be determined by the joint Council of Ministers of the ACP-EC, immediately after the signing of the Cooperation Agreement.

Abuja (Nigeria) hosted the 30th session of the joint Assembly of the ACP-EC on March 20 – March 23, 2000. A number of issues were considered, among which – the influence of the globalization process on the development of the Third World countries, the strategy of relations with the WTO, prevention and settlement of armed conflicts, amplification of the Assembly's role in the system of the EU-ACP relations, etc. Representatives of the ACP countries voiced their concern about the difficulties which recently emerged, in the course of support by the European Union of the developing states of region. Notably it has been remarked that, despite the trade preferences regime established for the ACP states, the share of their export to the EU-markets declined from 6.7% in 1976 to 2.8% in 1999. According to analyses conducted by the representatives of the ACP countries, 70% of the aid allocated by the EU to the economical development of the region's states returns to Europe one way or another. Concurrently, it was emphasized, that combating corruption and establishment of a good governance regime in the region's states still remain the requisite condition for granting them financial and technical assistance[9].

In a number of reports it has been pointed out that globalization in the currently existing forms is not a common weal, since many countries of the third world are indeed unable to compete with the economically developed countries. The WTO Conference in Seattle has shown that globalization does not in the least resolve all the problems, as it does not take into consideration the real interests of the developing countries. The Assembly participants see a possible outlet in the form of "organized globalization" with a "human face", namely a process which would allow the less-developed countries to gain significant advantages and privileges, without canceling the universal objectives and problems per se.

The EU and ACP countries were prompted to undertake a number of combined steps to this end. The first of them was the support of the demand to give up observing the WTO rules, submitted for consideration to the joint EU-ACP Council on February 29, 2000. John Horn, the President of the Council of ACP countries, pointed out that EU and ACP states in conjunction with the friendly Third World countries constitute more than three quarters of all the WTO member states (101 states of the 135 joined this organization), and called upon the Assembly to pass a resolution supporting this demand.

Issues regarding the allocation of financial and humanitarian aid by the European Union were considered at the Assembly. With regard to a concern voiced by some ACP states in connection with the cancellation of the STABEX and SYSMIN systems, Germany's representative A. Schremm pointed out that the various mechanisms stabilizing the export of natural resources to the EU markets would continue to function in the common framework of economic-aid. According to him, a total amount of €23 billion at the disposal of the EU for providing assistance to development of the region's countries would allow the EU to increase constantly the scales of annual financial and technical support rendered to the ACP states[10].

On June 23, 2000, at the 25th ministerial EU-ACP meeting in Cotonou, capital of Benin, a new partnership agreement between the EU and the ACP states was signed, determining the principles of cooperation of the parties for the next 20 years. The agreement received the official name "Partnership agreement between the African, Caribbean, and Pacific states on the one hand, and the European Union and its member states, on the other", and the less formal name – the Cotonou Agreement. The momentous event was timed to take place on the 25th anniversary of these conventions.

One of the basic goals of the Cotonou Agreement is a gradual and harmonious integration of the ACP countries into the world economy system, based on consolidation of regional integration processes within the ACP group itself. The basic principles of cooperation – respect of human rights, democratic norms, supremacy of law as well as the good governance regime – are complemented in the agreement by a political dialogue between the partners, which is now a major factor for granting financial aid by the EU. Important innovations are differentiation of aid, forming and development of civil society, encouragement of the private sector as well as support of the projects dealing with environmental preservation and mining operations. The agreement provides for a step-by-step process of transition towards the new trade regime that is no longer based on unilateral preferences, but gradually forms a system based on the principles of reciprocity. The regional economic cooperation agreements, which come into force in 2008, are to become the stages of this process, by preparing the creation of free economic zones in 2020. However, the less-developed ACP states, which are not ready to sign regional agreements, shall continue to benefit from the preferential regime.

The European Development Fund (EDF) is the main instrument for providing Community assistance for development cooperation under the Cotonou Agreement. The 10th EDF covers the period from 2008 to 2013 and has been allocated € 22.7 billion; it was established between the EU Member States by Internal Agreement. In comparison to the 9th EDF which covered the period 2000 to 2007, the initial amount available has increased by almost 65 % (the 9th EDF was initially allocated € 13.8 billion for 2000-2007)[11].

The 24th meeting of ACP-EU economic and social interest groups dealing with the implementation of the Cotonou Agreement, was held in Brussels on June 28–30, 2005. The participants noted the continued challenges to the development of ACP countries and stressed the necessity to rapidly address the low levels of investment, education/vocational training and employment in ACP countries. The participants welcomed the revisions to the Cotonou Agreement signed at the meeting of the ACP-EC Council of Ministers on 24 and 25 June 2005. A further focus lies on regional integration and sustainable development. On the topic of regional integration and sustainable development, the delegates stressed that priority should be assigned to the following aspects:
- The promotion of sustainable rural development
- The opportunities of sustainable tourism
- The threats of global climate change
- The necessity for the sustainable use of natural resources
- The challenge of HIV/AIDS, malaria and tuberculosis

• The importance of education and human resource development
• The promotion of gender equality

The first session of the Joint EU-ACP Parliamentary Assembly, held in Brussels from October 9 to 12, 2000, became the basic event which determined the nature of relations of the EU with the ACP states in the autumn of 2000. A wide range of issues of economic and political nature as well as environmental and health protection problems were considered at the session.

Four resolutions were adopted at the meeting: on the reform of the banana import regime, on rum and sugar trade as well as on relations with the WTO.

The assembly appealed to the industrialized countries of the north to open up their markets to the developing countries, to suspend the increase of tariffs, and to grant immediate free access to their markets to the export production of the 48 poorest countries of the region. Other suggested measures included: redistribution of grants in favor of agricultural export, cancellation of all the tariff and non-tariff barriers. It was also suggested that an opportunity be considered to set up international arbitration on issues of re-scheduling or cancellation of debts of the developing countries in cases when the indebtedness can hamper the normal functioning of the social welfare system. The delegates declared the necessity of introducing capital migration tax.

The session's work also brought to light the problems of health protection, notably the need for activization of the struggle against AIDS and malaria. A special resolution was adopted, calling upon the EU member states to increase the volume of financing and to provide political support to the programs aimed at the development of medicine in the region, among them educational programs, research and systematic observations as well as further training of medical staff. One of the major measures proposed was an essential reduction of medicine prices so as to provide the poorest population with an opportunity to receive medical care.

The assembly passed some resolutions on social affairs, among them resolutions regarding the role of women in the society, social development, human trafficking, problems of the non-industrial sector and fishery, problems of migration streams and distribution of aid for the social and economic development of the ACP countries.

A discussion about the issues of globalization revealed essential disagreements in the positions of the EU and the ACP states. Germany's representatives, in particular insisted on the "lack of understanding" and on the "underestimation" of the advantages of globalization by the developing countries of the region, whereas the latter drew attention to the discrepancy between the various directions of this process, leading, in their opinion, to the establishment of a kind of technological apartheid system, thus leaving the developing countries on the back seat of the world economic development. In all probability, the disputes on globalization are going to become one of the most serious stumbling-blocks on the way to realization of a new pattern of the EU-ACP cooperation[12].

The so-called Ministerial week of the ACP member states was held in December 2000 in Brussels. The meeting of trade ministers of the ACP countries selected the issue of the conclusion of Regional Economic Partnership Agreements (REPA) between the separate ACP and EU states under a multilateral system as one of the most important topics for discussion. Although the Cotonou Agreement, as an evolutionary continuation of the Lomé conventions, once again positioned the ACP group as a conglomerate of states united by common interests, a tendency towards diversification in the relations of the EU with various regional associations of countries within the ACP as well as with separate members of this group, was traced rather clearly. Thereupon the pattern of relations of the EU with the region's least developed countries which are to benefit from trade preferences in their entry to the markets of united Europe, acquires special significance. At the meeting, the issues of investment in the economy of the ACP states were broached, as well as regional integration and cooperation within the ACP and the need for amplification of the institutional potential of the ACP. The EU's standpoint as to the issues of increase of trade cooperation with the ACP group, stated at the meeting, adds up to an attempt to make the ACP capable of participating more fully in the world trade liberalization, both with the help of the Cotonou

Agreement and using the opportunities emerging during the negotiations with the WTO[13].

The second session of the Joint EU-ACP Parliamentary Assembly was held at Libreville (Gabon) from March 19–30, 2001. Issues of security, creation of the conditions facilitating the access of the ACP countries to the latest information technologies, the urgent threat of export of meat products infected by Bovine Spongiform Encephalopathy (BSE), or the so-called "mad cow" disease, in the context of trade interrelations of the EU and the ACP, the new "everything but arms" initiative and its influence over the export of the ACP countries, migration policies, racism, and even the consequences of use of impoverished uranium ammunition during the war on the Balkans were brought up for discussion at the session.

The implementation of the Cotonou Agreement and a reform of the administrative structure of economic aid granted by the European Union, undertaken by the Commission, aroused the main discussion. The fact that the Cotonou Agreement had been by then ratified only by 15 parliaments of the ACP countries and not ratified by any parliament of the EU member states aroused special concern of the delegates. Concurrently, fruitful consultations with a number of international agencies, including the World Bank, were conducted in several strategic directions, such as combating poverty, which was purported to be one of the major goals of the Agreement. The delegates resolved that it was necessary to reform the methods of work of the Joint EU-ACP Parliamentary Assembly so as to transform it into a full-fledged parliamentary body and to implement the scheduled strategy more efficiently. In order to accomplish this goal it is necessary for all the delegates to be members of national parliaments or of the European Parliament. Reduction of plenary sessions and parallel activation of work in committees and commissions to become the second major direction of reforms. Creation of three working groups (Conflict Prevention, Agriculture, and Health Protection) at the Parliamentary Session became the first practical step towards the realization of the idea. The German delegates also supported the cancellation of voting in various boards and the introduction of a system reflecting the political diversification in the ACP states, similar to the system of the European parties, by including opposition representatives in the ACP countries' delegations, and, as far as possible, by the association of the delegates to Assembly on the basis of their political convictions. The suggestion to hold the Assembly session annually in Europe, in one of capitals of the EU member states, was recognized as showing considerable promise. The assembly passed a number of important resolutions, one of them concerning the negotiations for acceptance to the WTO. Critical remarks regarding the new trade agreements between the ACP and the EU, based on cancellation of tariff barriers, were voiced at the Assembly. It was emphasized that the difference in level of economic development of the trading partners was putting them into wittingly unequal conditions, and that those contracts in their given form did not in the least contribute to the accomplishment of one of the basic goals of the Cotonou Agreement, namely the eradication of poverty in the region's countries[14].

The 16th session of the ACP-EU Joint Parliamentary Assembly was held on 24–28 November 2008 in Port Moresby, Papua New Guinea. The JPA debated the EU's economic partnership agreement with the Pacific region, passed resolutions on the political crises in Mauretania and Zimbabwe, and adopted reports on protecting civilians, aid effectiveness and child labour. The Port Moresby Declaration, adopted at the session, stressed that the world financial crisis should not be used to justify cuts in development aid to the Third World countries. The Declaration called the EU Member States to honour their official development assistance commitments – i.e. 0.56% of gross national income by 2010 and 0.7% by 2015.

The declaration also calls on the international community to reform and regulate the global financial system to guarantee transparency and ensure developing nations have a greater say.

"If the strongest economies in the world need economic stability – and they do – the weaker ones need economic dependability", commented JPA Co-President Glenys Kinnock.

The Assembly debated the EU's economic partnership agreements (EPAs) with Third World countries; the key issues debated were the rate at which "interim" versions of these agreements are being signed, whether or not services and intellectual property protection should be built into them, and whether the European Parliament should give its assent, in spring 1999, to their taking effect. The next, 17th session of the ACP-EU JPA is scheduled to take place in Prague (Czech Republic) from 4 to 9 April, 2009.

The implementation of the Cotonou Agreement – a framework agreement regulating the entire multiformity of EU links with 77 ACP states – was the EU's core of activity concerning this region in 2001–2002. The implementation of the Cotonou Agreement was conducted against the background of protractions on the part of the European partners with regard to the agreement ratification. Germany ratified the agreement in February 2002. On October 14, 2002, Glenys Kinnock, the co-chairman from the EU of the Joint EU-ACP Parliamentary Assembly, addressed the heads of states and governments of the three remaining countries which had not ratified the agreement – Italy, Belgium, and the Netherlands – with a request to accelerate the process. Nevertheless, all the agreement clauses, with the exception of financial provisions, went into effect at the beginning of 2002 by way of adopting transitional subordinate legislations by the participating countries. The uncompleted ratification of the agreement froze the means of the 9th European Development Fund (2000–2005), in which €12 billion was assigned for direct aid to the ACP states, and €1.7 billion – for the projects of the European Investment Bank.

The delayed ratification of the agreement gives grounds to a conclusion that one of its pillars – "cooperation in the name of development" – wound up on the back seat of the mutual EU-ACP relations in 2001–2002. It is also confirmed by the closing of the EU diplomatic missions and representations in nine of the ACP states.

Among the three bases of the Cotonou Agreement – political dialogue, cooperation aimed at development, and economic cooperation – the latter took priority from 2001–2002. The drafting of Economic Partnership Agreements (EPA) became the main element of implementation of this direction. EPAs are a medium-term alternative to the existing unilateral system of preferential trade applied between the EU and the ACP since the mid-1970s. The new trade order, directed at qualitatively new relations between the EU and the ACP, should satisfy the WTO's norms on the one hand, and protect the countries of the region from the negative consequences of a prompt liberalization of their trade regimes, on the other. The ACP countries secured themselves such protection at the 4th conference of the WTO countries at the level of heads of states and governments, held on November 9–13, 2001 at Doha (Qatar). Having demonstrated an unprecedented high level of intra-group unity, the ACP states achieved the decision that the rules of preferential trade between the EU and the ACP group would apply untill the end of 2007 (for trade in bananas – untill the end of 2005) – the moment when they are to be replaced by economic partnership agreements. On the other hand, it was assumed that even after 2007 the integration of the ACP countries into the system of world trade would occur on the basis of a flexible and asymmetric approach (as to time and economy sectors) to the least developed countries of the group (half of the 77 ACP states). It should be remarked, however, that the division of the ACP states into the least developed and other countries is rather conditional, since the cumulative share of all the ACP states in the world trade amounts to 0.05%.

According to the EU's strategy, economic partnership agreements are to be concluded between the EU and regional integration groups (in the first stage – free-trade zones) of the ACP states. According to the European commission's outlook, improvement of the trade balance between the North and the South is impossible without intensification of economic ties down the South-South line. Practically immediately after the signing of the Cotonou Agreement in June 2000, the ACP countries were offered to determine within the group those geographical formations with which new commercial agreements are to be made. By September 27, 2002 – the moment of official opening of negotiations on EPA – the ACP states succeeded in forming only two regional trade groups: ECOWAS and Mauritania (representing Western Africa), and the Economical and Monetary Community of Central

Africa and São Tomé (representing Central Africa). Discussions proceeded about who would represent Eastern and Southern Africa. Concurrently it was determined that the Republic of South Africa would not become a participant of the EPA owing to the fact that a bilateral agreement on trade, cooperation and development had been signed between it and the EU. The uncertainty with regard to the ACP regional free-trade zones does not yet threat to founder the EPA negotiations. The fact is that at the suggestion of the ACP countries negotiations were to be conducted in two stages: from September 2002 untill September 2003 and from September 2003 untill the end of 2007. At the first stage the ACP countries would act as a single player and work towards an accord with the EU on the basic rules of the new trade system, common for the entire region. The second stage of negotiations is concerned with the sub-regional level, the plane of specific issues: sensitive products of sub-regions, terms of the tariff barriers dismantling, warranties and indemnifications of the outlay regarding tariff liberalization in the Intra Regional Trade.

Negotiations on the EPA are conducted at the level of ambassadors (consultations) and ministers (decision-making). Six working groups have been established: on common problems of market access; agriculture; trade and services; competition, standardization, and certification; cooperation with the purposes of development; and legal affairs. The first two months of negotiations passed arduously: the basic line of "watershed" between the EU and the ACP revealed itself. The EU presses for an accelerated development of market structures prior to abolishing the mutual trade barriers of the ACP countries. "Opening up the markets without first creating them does not make any sense", – thus G.Mayer, a member of the EU Commission on trade on behalf of Germany, comments the EU standpoint. In their turn the ACP states urge the EU to highlight the compensatory aspects of the introduction of new trade regimes and the support of structural transformations in the economies of the ACP countries[15].

The meeting of ministers of the ACP states (December 11–12, 2002, Brussels) brought about a lot more practical feedback than the session of the Parliamentary Assembly. Issues of protecting sugar and

34

tuna exports from the ACP states to the EU were discussed at the meeting in the light of renewed criticism from a number of the ACP states at the address of the conditions of implementation of the preferential trade regime of the EU. The Council welcomed the EU's initiative to ease the indebtedness of certain ACP states in its resolution on financial development, but considered the number of states falling under the action of this plan to be insufficient.

At the first ongoing stage of negotiations on economic partnership between the regional groups of the ACP countries and the EU (September 2002 – September, 2003), the parties continued to discuss the objectives of the future Economic Partnership Agreements (EPA), the means of their accomplishment as well as the agenda of the second stage of negotiations (September 2003 – end of 2007). By the middle of February 2003, certain subjects of the second stage of negotiations were agreed upon, namely market access, trade, services, pharmaceutical goods, fishery products, and legal affairs[16].

The Cotonou Agreement came into force on April 1, 2003, clearing the way for the application of means of the first financial protocol covering a 5-year-period, as of March 5, 2000, and having the budget of €13.5 billion. No progress was observed in the spring regarding the economic partnership agreements (EPA), about which the ACP and the EU had conducted discussions since September 2002. As well as at the previous stage, the parties failed to reach a compromise about the methods of accomplishment of the stated goals – development, eradication of poverty, integration of the region into the world economy. The ACP states insist that development can be achieved by the accelerated build-up of production factors in the region (which in its turn is attainable by way of attracting direct financial investments); by the proper supply of the ACP group with the necessary foodstuffs, medicines, materials, and accessories; by a revision of the current WTO rules making allowance for the region's specific situation. As far as the European Union is concerned, it considers liberalization of trade, notably between the ACP states, to be the only efficient tool of development. In internal discussions the economic partnership agreements are with increasing frequency referred to as "trade" or "commercial agreements". An indicative declaration of the committee of ambassadors of the ACP countries of April 11, 2003 relates, in particular: "… every time we try to discuss development, or agriculture as one of its areas, the Europeans refuse to seek resolution of certain issues".

It is obvious that the EU is trying to reduce its specific obligations to the minimum in relation to the ACP states as a group. It is also confirmed by the fact that Brussels does not intend to continue the first phase of negotiations pending the settlement of all the issues. At different times the Commission members Paul Nelson and Helmut Mayer declared that in September 2003 the EU would commence the second phase of negotiations with those ACP integration groups which were ready. The Economic Community of West African States ECOWAS has expressed such readiness, though so far informally. It should be pointed out that the position of ECOWAS seriously undermines the internal solidarity of the ACP group.

The scale of divergences between the parties affected the results of the Brussels meeting of the Council of Ministers of the ACP-EC, held from May 14–15, 2003. The ACP and the EU failed to prepare a draft of the joint position for the meeting of states – participants of the WTO in Cancun. At a ministerial meeting of the WTO in Cancun, the ACP and the EU were planning to discuss the disagreements regarding the EPAs, despite having prepared extremely open and detailed platforms in advance.

The meeting of the Council of Ministers of the ACP-EC was conducted in the presence of delegates from the 10 EU applicant countries; one of the items on the agenda of the Council's meeting was the consequences of the EU expansion for the ACP states. According to the official sources' version, the Council "relieved the concern of the ACP countries about their interests being moved into the background" in view of the EU's expansion[17].

Summarizing this section of the current research, the authors of this monograph have arrived at the conclusion that in the last decade, Germany entertained relations with the African states within the framework of the concerted EU-ACP policies, playing quite an active part in the formation of the latter. Hereinafter the authors of this work recapitulate the main principles of development of Germany's relations with the African states.

1. Germany was one of the initiators of giving economic-aid (and in a wider sense, development of economic cooperation) to the developing countries, including Africa, conditional upon fulfillment of some political (or "humanitarian-democratic", as the authors of the idea formulated it) requests.

2. Germany pressed for the establishment of the good governance regime including, among other things, combating corruption up to suspending aid in case of infringement by African leaders, of the principle of respect for human rights and of the basic democratic freedoms.

3. Germany, acting in accord with the other EU countries, sought the implementation of temporary restrictions on the existence of trade preferences (not longer than 5–8 years).

4. From Germany's standpoint the key elements of the future partnership pattern are the increase of the role of civil society, of the private sector, and of social partners, namely socio-economic innovations in particular.

5. Germany in most cases appeared less prone to compromises than all the other EU participants on issues regarding facilitated access to the markets of the European states for cheap agricultural production from African countries, protecting the interests of its own agricultural producers.

6. Germany took a rather hard line on issues of providing assistance, emphasizing that in order to obtain such help, a combination of a number of factors was necessary, including such not the least important one, as active efforts of the would-be recipients of the EU's economic-aid. In the opinion of German experts, the concept of economic, financial, and technical support of the ACP countries by the European states has to undergo significant changes. The former practice of granting aid to all the countries requesting was abandoned. Now the receipt of European credit is conditional upon the fulfillment of a number of political demands.

7. Germany supports a flexible individual approach to partnership between the EU and the ACP states. Though the system of trade prefer-

ences is to be cancelled, the individual approach could allow the prevention of discrimination of the economically least developed countries of the region. Germany shall prepare ground for the conclusion of regional cooperation agreements; however, all the ACP countries should individually and voluntarily decide whether to conclude such agreements with the EU, depending on their opportunities.

8. A tendency towards diversification in the relations of the EU with the various regional associations of countries within the ACP as well as with separate members of this group has been traced rather clearly.

1.2. Political context and regulatory framework of Germany's commercial and economic relations with the African states of the Mediterranean

By the mid-1990s, the Mediterranean policy became one of the priority trends of the EU's activity. The Barcelona process, that is, expansion of cooperation of the EU member states with the so-called "third" Mediterranean countries (North Africa and the Middle East), is currently an essential factor influencing the system of international relations in the extensive region at the junction of three continents – Europe, Africa, and Asia. So what are the reasons underlying the EU's close attention to the Mediterranean region? What are the stages of development of the EU's Mediterranean policies? What are the today's specifics of these policies? What are the future prospects? What is the role of Germany in this process? This section of the monograph contains attempts to answer these basic questions.

As it was remarked in the previous section, the differentiated approach underpins Germany's economic relations with African countries. Germany undoubtedly develops its contacts, both political and economic ones, with all the countries of the continent; however, some African states are included in Germany's sphere of special interests, which becomes apparent by way of high intensity of trade and economic ties between them.

Countries of North Africa occupy a special place in the relations between the EU and the African continent, accounting for approximately 40% of the total turnover of the European states with Africa.

Germany is not an exception to the rule: the Arab Republic of Egypt and Tunisia are major trading partners in Africa behind the SRA. In 2002 they were among the 50 major external economic partners of reunified Germany, ranking respectively 43rd and 47th in the list[18]. The German-Libyan and German-Algerian economic relations have also intensified significantly since Libya and Algeria are the major suppliers of oil and gas to Germany.

The necessity for the EU, including Germany, to include the Mediterranean direction in their spectrum of activity is explained by a number of both objective and subjective reasons.

• **Geographical position.** All of the North African states lie in close proximity to the EU countries – they are divided only by the Mediterranean Sea. This facilitates contacts between them, which allows, in particular, to save on travel costs.

• **Stable political situation.** The governments of Egypt, Tunisia, and Morocco have ensured socio-political stability, which is a prerequisite for stable economic development, for a long time (more than 10 years). Algeria and Libya make an exception; however, the situation in these countries has also become more controllable in the last 2–3 years. The civil war in Algeria has stopped, and economic sanctions against Libya have been lifted. The aftermath of war in Iraq, the Palestinian problem and a number of other factors can undoubtedly blow up the peace in the region; however, the degree of development of state institutes in these countries in comparison to many states of Tropical Africa, where practical government bodies are absent, gives hope of a predictable, if not optimistic, way of evolution of the political situation.

• **Economic growth, reforms and economic liberalization.** Economic reforms were carried out in all the countries of North Africa in the 1990s, aimed at modernizing the economies, forming national markets, structural shifts in the national economies, privatizing public property, liberalizing trade, stabilizing the financial situation, and enhancing economic growth. Egypt, Tunisia, and Morocco have attained a resounding success therein. The successful advance of these countries on their way to becoming market economies facilitates their integration into the world economy and serves as an objective foundation for the development of commercial and economic relations with the EU.

According to the World Bank development indicators, the rate of economic growth in the Middle East and North Africa region grew from 3.2% in 2000 to 5.8% in 2007 (compared to 3.5% and 6.2% in sub-Saharan Africa). Per capita income in the MENA region, calculated by the World Bank according to the Atlas method (current US$) amounted to $1640 in 2000 and $2794 in 2007, e.g. $2090/$3200[19] for Tunisia, and $1610/$3620 for Algeria (compared to $483/$952 in sub-Saharan Africa in the years 2000/2007 respectively). The inflation rate in the MENA region accounted for 4.9% in 2000 and 4.6% in 2007 (compared with 6.1% and 6.5% in sub-Saharan Africa in the same years). The total external debt of the MENA countries in 2000 and 2007 accounted for $138,6 million and $145,6 million respectively ($211,7 million and $193,5 million for sub-Saharan Africa). The average life expectancy in the MENA region reached 68 years in 2000 and grew up to 70 years in 2006 (49 and 50 years in sub-Saharan Africa).

Thus, the relative economic stability inherent in the majority of countries of North Africa fostered the inflow of investments from the EU countries, including Germany, and expanded the opportunities for inter-regional cooperation.

• **Development of the industrial, social, and informational infrastructure.** All the countries of the North African region have developed infrastructure by African yardsticks: modern highways, railway communication, airports, marine and river transport, and a modern hotel service system.

The system of public health services is more developed in all the states of North Africa than in Tropical Africa; moreover, many of the countries of the region, for example, Egypt, have achieved relative success in the production of modern medicines. The education system in North Africa is closer to the European one; furthermore, children study a foreign language at secondary schools. The level of higher education, notably in Egypt, is also high enough to permit the training of experts in compliance with international demand. Thus, according to the latest census in Egypt, the share of the illiterate population over 10 years of age did not exceed 49.5% in the countryside, and 26.6% in the towns. Thus, in Cairo and Alexandria the literacy rate among the population made up approximately 80% by 2000. Within that period, the share of people with secondary education reached 41% in towns and 29% in the countryside, whereas the share of students and graduates went up to almost 13% for the urban and 3.7% for the rural population[20].

The total number of pupils in the country increased from 8.7 million in 1982 to 17.9 million in 2000, while the number of students in the same period – from 709 thousand to 1,670 thousand.

Availability of modern communication technology is one of the major conditions for the development of inter-state trade and economic ties in the 21st century. In this regard the North African states are inferior only to the SAR.

Thus, according to such an indicator as the number of telephones per 1,000 of population, the North African countries outnumber the sub-Saharan African countries by a factor of five (100 and 20 respectively). As regards the number of mobile phones, the spread between these groups is slightly lower, nevertheless it is double (30 and 15 respectively). Thus, the improved communication opportunities of the North African states facilitate the interrelations between the business partners of Europe and this region of Africa.

At the end of the 1990s there was a "mobile phones boom" in the Arab Republic of Egypt as well as in a number of other African countries: the number of users surged from 200,000 in early 1999 to 3.4 million in 2001; 12 million in 2005, and 17 million in 2007, according to the Egyptian Ministry of Communications and Information Technology (MCIT)[21]. The Ministry of Communications and Information Technology (MCIT) was created in Egypt in 1999. In August 2000, the government allocated $1 billion to the development and modernization of the country's communication systems. The information sector was named among the priority development sectors, while the preferential system of taxation became highly attractive to foreign investors[22].

By 2000 the number of host computers in Egypt surged to 57 thousand, whereas the number of users reached 250 thousand people[23]. These are the highest indicators throughout Africa (SAR excluded). For all that, as to the number of the country's inhabitants per host computer, which in the Arab Republic of Egypt reached 1123 people in 2000, Egypt differs favorably from its North African neighbors – Tunisia and Morocco, where the corresponding figures in the same period constituted 1371 and 1390 people[24].

The number of personal computers in Egypt at the end of the 1990s calculated per 1,000 inhabitants was under 8, in Algeria – 5, in Tunisia – 10, in Morocco – 4. As to the countries of Tropical Africa, by the indicator in question they were considerably inferior to the countries of North Africa. Thus, in Benin the figure was under – 0.9, in Mali – 0.6, Guinea – 0.3, in Uganda – 1.4, Ghana – 1.6, in Niger – 0.2, in Tanzania – 1.6.

Two hundred state information centers servicing the executive and legislative power in the ARE, 217 economic and social information centers, 311 urban, 169 regional, and 916 rural information centers as well as 645 special information departments, aimed at providing and stimulating the growth of information technologies locally, operated in the countries of North Africa in 2002[25].

• **Development of tourism**. The countries of North Africa, primarily Egypt, Tunisia, and Morocco – are centers of attraction for tourists from Europe, including Germany. Annually approximately 100 thousand Germans visit these states[26]. A personal acquaintance with a country gives the best insight as to its opportunities and prospects of development. Many professional contacts of German entrepreneurs with the representatives of local business started after such tourist trips.

• **Migration.** Migration of Africans to Europe, including Germany, became one of the most pressing problems at the end of the 20th – beginning of the 21st century. The issues regarding migration will be considered in more detail in the 3rd chapter of this research. It should be stressed that a significant number of African immigrants come to European countries from North Africa due to geographical proximity,

42

linguistic affinity as well as to a number of historical preconditions. In the last decade, Germany became one of the most attractive recipient countries for immigrants from North Africa. Issues of regulating migration inflows from this region are one of the most urgent today and require both drafting of concerted approaches of the member nations of the European Union and allowing for the local specificity of the donor and host countries.

• **Development and perfection of the investment legislation**. The investment legislation passed in most countries of North Africa operates in the interests both of the national economy and of the Western investors. The most liberal investment legislation was adopted in Egypt and Tunisia. Thus, in Egypt foreign capital is completely secured against nationalization. Foreign capital enjoys special privileges in 16 branches of the economy, such as cultivating the land, poultry farming, cattle breeding, industry, construction, tourism, processing and storage of agricultural commodities, marine and air transport, housing construction, real estate operations, oil refining and transportation, construction of hospitals and medical centers, water-pump stations, venture capital, development of computer technologies, social sphere, and securities market. In that way all the companies operating in these spheres (the foreign ones included) are exempted from profit tax for five years. The foreign capital invested in new industrial areas and new urban centers, is exempted from profit tax for 10 years. Should foreign companies choose areas outside the Nile valley as their sphere of action, then the grace period is extended to 20 years. Companies whose activity is not related to priority branches of economy can also obtain similar privileges. All the new companies, including the foreign ones, with a number of workers over 50 people, benefit from a 5-year-exemption from all taxes.

In Tunisia, tax privileges lasting up to 10 years are accorded to export companies. The import of materials and equipment is exempted from taxes. Investments on preferential terms can be made in the tourism sphere, including construction of hotels, health protection, education, environmental protection, waste processing, science, and new technologies. Thus, the inflow of foreign capital is welcomed in most

43

spheres of the national economy, as it is laid down in the investment legislation of the respective North African country.

All the above-listed factors indicate the necessity of drafting special principles of interrelations between the EU countries and the North African nations. Therefore, while the evolution of interrelations with the countries south of Sahara was basically governed by the Lomé conventions, and at the present time – by the Cotonou Agreement on the basis of the united approach to the ACP states, Germany's political and economic cooperation with the region of North Africa is carried out both in the framework of the Barcelona process and by the conclusion of bilateral agreements on cooperation in the socioeconomic sphere.

The EU's Mediterranean policy is rooted in the '50s, when the European powers, having embarked on the path of organizational rapprochement and integration, were confronted with the collapse of their colonial empires and started to seek new forms of interrelations with their former colonies.

This found the most precise expression in the Treaty of Rome, signed by the Federal Republic of Germany, Belgium, France, Italy, Luxembourg, and the Netherlands in Rome in 1957[27].

According to the treaty, the Community's activity provided for the "association with the overseas countries and territories with a view to increase trade and jointly encourage economic and social development". One cannot but admit that the issue on association was worked out in the Treaty in great detail. Thus, it determined the nature of trade regime, approach to such problems as capital investment, right to residence and to economic activities, customs duties, order of preparation of subsequent agreements, and ascertaining of the availability of "specific conditions and procedures necessary for the association between the countries and territories and the Community"[28]. One can infer from the text of the document that as applied to the Mediterranean, the issue at hand was an opportunity of association with those countries and territories which maintained "special relations" with France and Italy.

Thus, the article 227 stipulated that the Treaty's general and special provisions (on the mobility of goods, agriculture, liberalization of services, competition rules, protective measures, and institutes) had applied to Algeria from the moment the Treaty came in force. The Protocol to the Treaty specified that some measures within the competence of the European Coal and Steel Community (ECSC) applied to Algeria[29].

The Appendix IV stipulated that the provisions of the part IV of the Treaty also applied to Mauritania (p. 481).

The Treaty's formulations concerning Libya are worth mentioning. Thus, the Declaration of Intentions specified the existence of "economic ties between Italy and the Kingdom Libya", the aspiration "to support and intensify the traditional trade flow between the Community's member states and the Kingdom Libya and to promote Libya's economic and social development". Thereupon the "readiness ... to propose to the Kingdom Libya to begin negotiations with a view to conclude a convention on economic association with the Community" was stated[30].

However, as is well known, after the revolution of September 1969 and the overthrow of the monarchy, upon Muammar al-Quaddafi's coming to power, the relations between the EU and Libya had worsened, so these provisions were not embodied.

Thus, one might consider that the Treaty of Rome formulated the basic objectives and problems of the EU in the Mediterranean region, laid down the basis for an action program in the Mediterranean direction, encouraged the growth of activity of the EU member states in the Mediterranean region.

However, the first trade agreements with the countries of the Southern Mediterranean (Morocco and Tunisia) were only signed in 1969. In the 1970s a number of agreements were concluded with Morocco, Algeria, Tunisia, Egypt, Jordan, Lebanon, and Syria, providing for the economic and financial cooperation and laying the foundation of the EU's policy aimed at integrating the region with the Community.

It is noteworthy that Germany's role in the development of relations with the countries of the Southern Mediterranean was absolutely special. Unlike England, France, and Italy, Germany had not possessed colonies on the territory of North Africa; the attitude of the local population of the countries in question towards Germany was therefore more loyal and friendly. Until recently Germany was confronted with the problem of African migration to a lesser degree than Italy, France, and Spain since the main flows were targeted at the three above-mentioned countries. Finally, Germany, as compared to other EU member states, disposed of a much higher economic potential and with it opportunities of financial injections into the economy of the Third World countries. Thus, Germany appeared from the outset in a more favorable position in comparison to other European states regarding the development of political, commercial, and economic relations with the states of North Africa.

One may assume that the declaration of a "new Mediterranean policy" (at that time a policy of Euro-Mediterranean cooperation and partnership) made by the EU in the 1990s, was affected by a number of factors.

Firstly, by that time the EU had turned into a powerful association of West-European states, some kind of a world centre exerting its force and influence over all the spheres of international life. The needs of its economic and political development required the expansion of the system of unions and interaction.

Secondly, the work towards the involvement of the "third" Mediterranean countries into its sphere of influence is determined by the necessity to withstand the competition with the US both on a global and regional scale. Establishing and consolidating integration groups in the Western hemisphere and in the Asian-Pacific region, the US are not less actively starting to outrun Western Europe on the Mediterranean direction.

Thirdly, as it has already been mentioned above, a number of destabilizing processes of the military-political and socioeconomic nature had expanded in the Mediterranean by that time, jeopardizing the further formation of the EU.

Moreover, the disintegration of the Soviet Union and the significant reduction of Russia's role in the life of the Mediterranean brought about a vacuum which required filling.

Within this policy the EU signed association agreements with Turkey, Cyprus, and Malta. Negotiations are being held regarding the opportunity of their possible accession to the EU as full members. A distinctive feature of the agreements of that period was that they provided a relatively free access of industrial production from the Southern Mediterranean to the EU market, although they limited the export of agricultural production to Europe, which competed with the similar production of the Northern Mediterranean EU member states. As indemnification, the South Mediterranean countries receive certain economic and financial aid.

The basic outlines of the actual Mediterranean policy of the EU were set out in the Maastricht Treaty which entered into force on 1 November 1993. The Treaty proclaimed "association with the overseas countries and territories" as one of the objectives of the Community's activity, having reinstated the formulation of the Treaty of Rome (the Single European Act. Treaty on the European Union. M., 1994, p. 53). The Declaration (no. 25) on representation of interests of the overseas countries and territories is attached to the Treaty; the relevant responsibilities of the European investment bank are formulated. The Maastricht Treaty, having essential significance for the further destiny of the European Union, also promoted the intensification of the EU activity in the Mediterranean direction. The meetings of the EU leaders in 1994 (Corfu and Essen) and in 1995 (Cannes) supported the "new Mediterranean policies".

However, the "Euro-Mediterranean conference" in Barcelona (November 27–28, 1996) was the major move in promoting the EU in the Mediterranean region, adopting a Declaration indicative of the success of the EU's "new Mediterranean policies" (see "Europe. Agence internationale d'information pour la presse". Bruxelles, 6 December 1995). Upon the completion of the conference, the EU Council, the EU Commission, and all the EU member states announced their approval of the Declaration's text.

The novelty of this document consists of the following. Firstly, none of the similar multilateral statements concerning the Mediterranean was ever signed by so many Ministers for Foreign Affairs. It was a Declaration of 27 states: the 15 EU member states and the 12 non-European Mediterranean ("third") states.

Secondly, the Declaration laid down a new, higher level of interrelations than previously. Henceforth they are to be referred to as the "Euro-Mediterranean partnership", established through the "consolidation of the political dialogue on a regular basis, the expansion of economic and financial cooperation with a greater focus on the social, cultural, and human dimensions".

Thirdly, such partnership was to become universal indeed. The Declaration's sections cover policy and security, economy and finance, social and humanitarian problems.

Finally, the Declaration was simultaneously a working program for the implementation of impressive projects, the main one being the creation of a free-trade zone in the Mediterranean by 2010.

Active work towards implementing the arrangements achieved at the Barcelona conference started immediately upon its completion. Already in January, 1995 the Presidency of the Council of the European Union accorded priority to the EU activity in the Mediterranean. Work in this area was particularly concrete and covered all the new trends stipulated by the Barcelona Declaration.

In terms of strengthening the regional security, work started to prepare offers to adopt the charter of peace and stability in the Euro-Mediterranean region, documents on "preventive diplomacy", to establish a Centre concerning the Mediterranean situation, a Euro-Mediterranean college of development and security, other arrangements of cooperation in the military-political sphere, among them measures of trust and openness (exchange of information about military expenditure, preliminary notification about military maneuvers, etc.).

A number of meetings on issues of economic cooperation were held at the ministerial level. Already at the first Euro-Mediterranean conference on power engineering a decision was made to set up the Euro-Mediterranean Energy Forum, and eventually the single Euro-Mediterranean power market. A transitional package is being worked out for activity under the conditions of the Euro-Mediterranean free-trade zone. Another notable achievement was the deployment of a system for financing the Euro-Mediterranean cooperation.

A number of important actions have been conducted to implement the Barcelona decisions in the field of ecology, culture, and tourism.

At the same time, the Euro-Mediterranean cooperation has encountered some real difficulties. Thus, the drafting of the Peace Charter was hampered by confrontational relations between the participant states (Turkey – Greece, Israel – Palestine, Arab nations – Israel). Difficulties of cooperation in economic terms lie in the fact that contractual bilateral relations between the EU and other participants (notably, the Arab nations) are now at different stages, whereas the leveling of these relations is progressing very slowly at the moment. There is no united opinion as to how to stop the growth of disproportions in the development of the Mediterranean North and South. The practical implementation of many seemingly up-and-coming projects has experienced difficulties in attracting investments, both from national capital and from abroad. The issue on deliveries of cheap agricultural production to the EU markets still remains unsettled. Germany has shown special concern in this regard.

These problems rose in all their magnitude before the second Euro-Mediterranean conference (held on April 15–16, 1996, in Malta) which, according to the organizers' intentions, should have totaled the first results of development of this new regional cooperation dimension. Owing to a small number of representative participants, the Malta conference turned out to be in a worse position than its forerunner in Barcelona. The Ministers for Foreign Affairs of Great Britain, Greece, Turkey, Portugal, and Austria did not attend the Malta conference. Nevertheless, Germany took a very active stand at that forum.

The conference failed to adopt a Joint declaration due to a collision between the West-European position, on the one hand, and the position of the "third" Mediterranean countries, on the other. While discussing military and political affairs (the Charter, military cooperation, etc.) the Arab states sharply criticized Israel and demanded of the conference to condemn its actions. In the sphere of economy, the Arab nations expressed in a harsh form, their discontent about the pace of development of the Euro-Mediterranean cooperation, accusing the EU of egoism and slow implementation of the measures agreed to in Barcelona. Only after the conference, the senior officials managed to draft the so-called joint "conclusions" based on the results of the conference. The idea of continued cooperation between the EU and the "third" Mediterranean countries was adopted as a foundation.

What set off the crisis that emerged in the system of Euro-Mediterranean cooperation?

It would seem that the EU strategy failed to take into account the role of foreign policy components in the Barcelona process to the right degree. While drafting the common regional principles of security and stability, no attention was paid within the relevant Charter to specific conflicts, for example, to the Middle East situation. A significant delay in the adoption of the MEDA Democracy Programme was the first signal of such miscalculation. Also, the preparation for the Malta conference was complicated due to a clash of positions between Israel and the Arab states. Already by the beginning of the conference it was clear that it was doomed to fail.

The crisis situation in the system of Euro-Mediterranean cooperation has also emerged due to the unsettled disagreements between the EU and a number of North African countries in the field of bilateral economic relations. Furthermore, the Arab nations are strongly critical of the EU activity which is frequently considered as infringing on the interests of the economies of the "third" Mediterranean states. They wish to get real benefits from the Euro-Mediterranean cooperation. A dangerous tendency for these countries is that their import to Europe is much less than the export of the EU countries to the southern and eastern Mediterranean. Thus, the export from Europe increased by 10% in 1995, whereas the import to Europe – only by 4%. ("Europe", March 3–4, 1997). Taking into account the measurement of the absolute figures of such a turnover, it would be discovered that the "third" Mediterranean countries are indeed in a difficult situation.

Finally, the social and humanitarian sphere was a weak point in the Euro-Mediterranean strategy of the EU. It has received insufficient attention, in comparison with the others, though such problems as migration and, especially the rights of immigrants on the European continent, are extremely topical in the opinion of the Arab nations.

One could assume that the Euro-Mediterranean cooperation shall nevertheless develop. In an environment where such phenomena as regionalism and integration walk hand in hand, increasingly gaining foothold in the world community, the Euro-Mediterranean cooperation has chances to advance. However, it is confronted with numerous difficulties. Much depends on how efficient the EU strategy will be and whether it succeeds in evaluating its blunders realistically and rectifying them.

The common principles of commercial and economic relations of the EU, including Germany, with the countries of North Africa are about the same as with the ACP states. Hence the first Africa-EU summit was held on April 3 and 4, 2000 in Cairo, it expanded the scales of cooperation of the EU with the countries of the region and designated the new prospects thereof. The EU partnership with the countries of Africa had born a regional character heretofore: the Barcelona process encompassed African countries north of the Sahara, whereas the Lomé conventions and the partnership Agreement that replaced them provided for cooperation with the continent's countries south of Sahara. The Cairo summit, which initiated the regular process of consultations between the EU and the African countries, was a result of the EU's readiness to proceed to the strategy of cooperation with Africa as a whole.

The summit was attended by Antonio Guterres – the acting (in early 2000) president of the European Council, the OAU president Abdelaziz Bouteflika; the president of Egypt (the host country), Mubarak; the president of France, Chirac; the chancellor of Germany, Schröder; as well as prime ministers of Spain and the Benelux countries. Romano Prodi, Poul Nilsen, Chris Patten, and Javier Solana participated in the summit on behalf of the EU.

A number of topical political and economic issues of the EU's interrelations with the countries of the African continent were considered at the summit. Three debate groups were generated to discuss economic and social affairs, issues of political dialogue, human rights, democracy, fair governance, and prevention of conflicts as well as of the common problems of development. At the same time, regional divergences of goals and tasks facing the EU's African partners persist in spite of a more global approach to cooperation. Thus, Egypt actively asserted its idea to establish denuclearized zones (primarily, in the Middle East), advanced by it previously under the Barcelona process. Concurrently, the ACP states demanded opening negotiations on restitution of the cultural valuables exported during the colonization to the European metropolitan countries. Almost all the African countries broached the subject of external debt to a greater or lesser extent. The European commission's representatives emphasized that the problem of indebtedness of the African countries to private creditors is to be settled within the framework of specialized agencies, notably the Paris Club.

For the African states the issue of institutionalizing the EU's cooperation with the countries of the continent was of fundamental importance. Representatives of these countries were pressing for continuity and regularity of such meetings, in order to boost the efficiency of the process launched in Cairo. Representatives of the EU, sharing the idea about the process continuity, avoided committing to regular EU-Africa summits. Nevertheless, one of the main results of the Cairo meeting was an arrangement to convene the second EU-Africa summit in 2003 in Europe.

At the Cairo meeting a joint declaration was adopted, which appeared, in fact, as a charter of the forthcoming cooperation between the EU and the countries of Africa. The establishment of a constant dialogue between the EU and Africa can be considered as the summit's main result, as it should help solve the issues of political nature, including those related to preventing and settling armed conflicts, which still present one the continent's most pressing problems[31].

Nevertheless, there is a difference between the specific substance of the current agreements and the organizational frameworks of the EU's and Germany's cooperation with the countries of the Mediterranean, due to, as it is shown above, the changed geopolitical environment and the history of relations formation.

Traditionally close and versatile trade and economic ties have developed between the EU and Maghreb (Morocco, Tunisia, and Algeria).

More than 55% of all the export of the Maghreb countries is accounted for by the EU member states (more than 30% of them – by Germany), which are the major buyers of oil and mineral oils, natural gas, phosphates, fruit and vegetables, seafood imported from Maghreb, as well as of some products of the manufacturing industry (notably the light and chemical industries). Concurrently, the EU member nations are Maghreb's largest suppliers of machines and equipment (where Germany is the absolute leader), vehicles and foodstuffs (grain, dairy products, etc.). The basic part of financial and technical aid received by the Maghreb countries, as well as of currency earnings from tourism and private transfers, originates from the EU.

In 1976, Germany signed working agreements within the European Economic Community, with Algeria, Morocco, and Tunisia, determining the main principles of the trade and economic ties renewed by the protocols. Since the moment of signing these agreements the Maghreb countries have granted Germany and other EU member states the most-favored nation treatment. The EU in its turn has afforded each of the Maghreb countries an opportunity to export agricultural products, raw material, semi-finished goods, and industrial products to the community markets without any duties or quantitative restrictions, under the existing cooperation agreements. Those agreements still exist on the whole; however, in many respects they increasingly acquire a declarative nature as they make a number of important exceptions: a quota on duty-free deliveries of some agricultural products is established, whereas the deliveries of textile goods and garments are subject to so-called "voluntary restrictions", agreed to with the Union's countries.

The Mediterranean policies were one of the lines along which the EU's and, primarily Germany's activity has considerably increased lately. The relevant accents emerged after the setup of the new structure of the European Commission, were contained in the speech of the European Commission member, Chris Patten, in Cairo on April 1, 2000. As appears from the statement, the EU's basic approaches to the problems of the Mediterranean add up to the following:

1. The Barcelona process is an axis around which the EU's foreign policy in the Mediterranean is deployed; the attention to this direction

is to be intensified, as the Mediterranean is a region of paramount significance.

2. Within the five year period real progress has been achieved, manifested through the following:

• The meetings within the Barcelona process became the only forums attended by all the 27 participating states even in the difficult stages of development of the peace process in the Middle East;

• The European import to the Mediterranean stands at more than €30 billion at present, i.e. approximately 47% of the total amount of import; the amounts of export are even higher: more than €63 billion of the Mediterranean export, which is approximately 52% of the total amount of export, are accounted for by the EU;

• Europe became the region's major donor; during the last five years the EU has invested more than €4.4 billion in the Mediterranean region, while the European Investment Bank has granted credits to the amount of €4.6 billion.

3. It is unacceptable that the EU's expansion into the Central and Eastern Europe would hamper the development of partnership with the Mediterranean countries;

4. Owing to the partnership with the Mediterranean countries, the processes initiated by the EU encompass altogether 500 million people; this shall require institutional changes;

5. Although under the Barcelona process such problems as modernization of the public sector, cancellation of trade barriers and coordination of trust measures are being successfully solved, there is nevertheless a number of problems which require much more attention than they receive nowadays. These are fostering trade in the South-South system, developing free-trade sub-regions; improving agriculture. There is evidence of insufficient financing, indistinct determination of the priority degree of the projects, and delayed implementation thereof. It is important to adopt effective measures to combat terrorism, illegal immigration, to prevent conflicts and secure human rights. The Charter for Peace and Stability in the Mediterranean has hitherto not been adopted.

6. A vital issue for Europe's Mediterranean policies is the development of the peace process in the Middle East, where the EU needs

close cooperation with the US. The EU has invested enormous political and financial resources in the solution of the region's problems. Since 1993 the EU has been the major donor of the Palestinian administration, since 1996 it has a special representative in the region. New financial investments in the Middle East peace process shall be required of the EU.

7. Consolidating the peace in the Balkans is unattainable without appropriate financial resources. The EU member states who reluctantly agree to new costs should comprehend this.

Chris Patten communicated that a document with an exposition of the EU's strategy for the Mediterranean would be prepared in the following months.

Alongside the development of new approaches to solving the problems of Euro-Mediterranean cooperation, the EU has concentrated its attention on stimulating activity in some specific areas of priority significance.

Thus, the Euro-Mediterranean Conference on Investment was held in Lisbon, on 28th February – 1st March, 2000; it was attended by more than 300 managers of banks, financial and industrial companies, in addition to the ministers and the heads of other departments of the countries participating in the Barcelona process. At the conference it was highlighted that European investments in the Mediterranean are smaller than in Asia, although the French Minister of Finance, Christian Sautter remarked, "The Euro-Mediterranean cooperation is a priority for the EU's foreign policy" and "bears a strategic character". The participants agreed to study the proposals put forward at the conference, including the ones on creating a network of guarantee agencies for the investors, establishing a secretariat of the Mediterranean Union, conducting a "virtual forum" to consider the opportunity of using new technologies in the region.

The scarcity of European investments in the economy of the southern Mediterranean was highlighted during the preparation of the 3rd Euro-Mediterranean Conference of Ministers for Industry, which convened on June 22, 2000 in Limassol (Cyprus); the previous ones were held in 1996 at Brussels and in 1998 in Austria. The lack of investments was appraised in May 2000 at the meeting of heads of industrial federations of the 27 countries participating in the Barcelona process as one of the main obstacles to the development of a "dialogue" between the industrial circles of the South and North Mediterranean.

It has been resolved, as one of the measures to enhance such dialogue, to set up a business network, UNIMED – an informal network consisting of groups of industrialists with a view to secure an exchange of information and experience. The European commission assumes the expenses of €2.5 million, the total cost of the project amounting to €3.4 million.

Measures are being discussed towards further increase of the efficiency of financial programs of the Euro-Mediterranean cooperation – MEDA. The demands to revise the rules by which these programs are implemented and criticism of the complex bureaucratic procedures reducing the efficiency of programs were voiced at a special meeting of the representatives of the European Parliament and European commission in March 2000. Chris Patten believes that the sums at MEDA's disposal are to be increased by 47%.

Prospects of development of the situation in the Mediterranean and in the world were considered at the Conference of Presidents of the Parliaments of the Euro-Mediterranean countries, held in May 2000 in Alexandria (Egypt). Special attention was paid to the struggle against terrorism.

The issues related to rendering dynamism to the Euro-Mediterranean process became a subject of consideration at the meeting of Ministers for Foreign Affairs of the 27 countries in Lisbon on May 25-26, which passed in a format of a free exchange of opinions "off the agenda". Given the new conditions in the region, both methods and objectives of the Euro-Mediterranean cooperation were discussed. However, cardinal conclusions were to be made only in November in Marseilles at the 4th Euro-Mediterranean conference (Barcelona IV)[32].

The adoption of a normative document – the "Joint strategy of the European Union for the Mediterranean region" – by the meeting of the European Council held on June 19–20, 2000, in Santa Maria da Feira (Portugal) became a major event in this trend. It is the third document of the "EU strategy" series; the previous ones were adopted for Russia and the Ukraine. It would seem that in comparison to them it is less specific, prevailed by conceptual positions rather than plans, instructions, and recommendations of practical nature.

The document comprises several sections. The first one – "Vision of the Mediterranean region by the European Union" – features the "strategic significance" and "vital importance" of the Mediterranean region for the EU, it states that a "prospering, democratic, stable region of security, with prospects connected to Europe, meets to the highest degree the interests of the EU and Europe at large".

The "Objectives" section, alongside such goals as "creating a space of peace and stability by way of partnership in the sphere of politics and security", "cooperative security in the region", "securing a partnership in the social, cultural, and humanitarian areas", highlights the necessity to increase the efficiency and the degree of impact of the EU's activity in the region.

Under the "Spheres of activity and specific initiatives" section, attention is focused on the issues of combating terrorism, organized crime, and drug traffic as well as on preventing and settling conflicts, supporting the campaign to ban anti-missile systems, antipersonnel (AP) mines, and upholding the provisions of the Ottawa convention.

A special significance is attributed to the EU's activity in the Middle East, which is to be transformed into a zone free of weapons of mass destruction in the future, whereas the current goal is to increase the efforts on participation in the peace process and to prepare the EU for actions in the Middle East after peace is established there.

In economic and financial terms, the EU's strategy consists of developing the dialogue and reaching agreements on association with the Mediterranean countries, liberalizing the movement of capital, fostering the mutual economic cooperation between the "third" Mediterranean countries, including within the framework of the Arab Maghreb Union and down the South-South line.

The two final sections are dedicated to administrative-organizational and protocol affairs.

Whereas the document on joint strategy is concerned with long-term indicators of the EU Mediterranean policies, the short-term intentions are contained in the "Working program of France holding the rotating European Union's presidency", France performing these functions from July 1 until December 31, 2000. The French party regards the development of the Euro-Mediterranean relations as the European Union's "key concern". France is going to bring order into the operation of the Mediterranean financial program – MEDA; the issues of the EU Mediterranean policies were to be considered completely at the 4th Euro-Mediterranean conference of Foreign Ministers of the 27 states (Barcelona IV), held on November 15–16, 2000, in Marseilles. It was expected that the text of the Charter of Peace and Stability in the Mediterranean had been already prepared by that time; the drafting of the charter had lasted for five years.

France sought to sign an association agreement between the EU and Egypt as well as to promote negotiations on similar agreements with Lebanon, Syria, and Algeria. Simultaneously it pressed for the opening of negotiations on agricultural issues with Tunisia, Morocco, and Israel.

In a series of major actions organized in summer 2000, one should single out the 3rd Euro-Mediterranean conference of ministers of industry (July, Cyprus), which approved the working program in the field of industrial cooperation. The program envisaged four priority groups: 1) promoting the attraction of investments in the region; 2) developing the innovation process as regards technologies and quality; 3) improving the mechanism of formation of the Euro-Mediterranean market; 4) developing the medium and small-sized business, and developing thereupon a relevant working program in 2001. The following conference was scheduled to take place in 2002 in Spain.

Contradictions between the EU member states in the issue of relation towards Libya still persisted by 2000. Although the "Joint strategy of the European Union for the Mediterranean region" acknowledges that such strategy applies to Libya too, Romano Prodi was nevertheless subjected to sharp criticism for sending, without coordination with the member states, an invitation to the Libyan leader Kaddafi to visit Brussels.

1.3. Institutional basis of cooperation and human capital formation in Africa[33]

Germany's trade and economic cooperation with the developing, including African, countries is implemented through a system of state, private, and public structures, each of them performing certain tasks and functioning in interaction with other agencies which pursue similar goals.

Germany's main public agency on trade and economic cooperation with foreign countries is the Federal Ministry for Economic Cooperation – Bundesministerium für wirtschaftliche Zusammenarbeit und Entwicklung (BMZ). The ministry was established in November, 1961, under a decision of the German government. At the celebration of the 40th anniversary of this state authority, BMZ's head Heidemarie Zeul pointed out that its main task had been and continued to be the struggle against the non-uniformity of economic development of the world's regions, struggle for social and political rights of peoples of different countries and for their global security[34]. BMZ's basic mission is to draft the principles of Germany's economic policy in the Third World countries. The ministry's activity is reduced to the following problems:

1. Analyzing the global economic situation.

2. Drafting bilateral and multilateral programs of Germany's cooperation with the third world countries.

3. Supporting the activity of non-governmental organizations (NGOs) in Germany's partner countries.

4. Supervising the implementation of the relevant programs and projects as well as the use of financial resources.

The Federal Ministry for Economic Cooperation and Development (BMZ) has some 600 employees. About 80 per cent of them are based at the Ministry's Bonn office, while the others work at the Berlin office. In April 2003, BMZ underwent a reorganization which brought about new structural divisions and reorganized the former ones. As of 2009, BMZ is headed by the Minister, Heidemarie Wieczorek-Zeul, the Parliamentary State Secretary, Karin Kortmann, and the State Secretary, Erich Stather. The Bonn office consists of the following Directorate-Generals:

• Directorate-General 1 (made up of 14 divisions) is primarily responsible for general administrative tasks, and for cooperation with civil society forces, including NGOs and political foundations. The division for evaluation and auditing reports directly to the Director-General. This Directorate-General is also responsible for the administration of the Bonn and Berlin offices.

• Directorate-General 2 (made up of 16 divisions) is responsible for development cooperation with countries and regions in Asia, Latin America and Europe and for peacebuilding, democratisation and the United Nations. It is responsible for basic policy work with the partner countries, political dialogue and determining the shape of bilateral cooperation. It coordinates and integrates all development policy measures and is responsible for the management and monitoring of all Financial and Technical Cooperation projects and programmes with individual countries.

• Directorate-General 3 (made up of 18 divisions) is responsible for cooperation with international organisations and for donor coordination. Responsibility for Africa and the Middle East has also been transferred to this Directorate-General, the aim being to ensure that cooperation with the individual countries in these regions is coordinated even more closely with the efforts of international institutions. Directorate-General 3 is headed by its Director-General, Dr. Michael Hofmann.

Mandate of the Ministry. As we stand at the beginning of the 21st century, the role of development policy has changed, partly as a reaction to the terrorist attacks of 11 September 2001. Today, development cooperation is seen as global structural and peace policy. It aims to help resolve crises and conflicts in a peaceful manner. It aims to help ensure that scarce resources are more equitably shared, and that our environment is preserved for coming generations. And it aims to help reduce global poverty.

In order to achieve these goals, development policy must target different levels. And of course we cannot lose sight of the fact that foreign policy, trade policy, security policy and development policy are today very closely linked. This makes the mandate of the Federal Ministry for Economic Cooperation and Development (BMZ) wide and varied.

Defining the fundamental principles of German development policy. The BMZ develops the guidelines and the fundamental concepts on which German development policy is based. It devises long-term strategies for cooperation with the various players concerned and defines the rules for implementing that cooperation. These are the foundations for developing shared projects with partner countries and international development organisations. All efforts are informed by the United Nations' Millennium Development Goals, which ambitiously aim to halve poverty in the world by 2015. The German government's contribution to the realisation of these goals is enshrined in its cross-departmental Program of Action 2015, for which the BMZ is the lead ministry.

Cooperation with partner countries. In political and financial terms, the main focus is on bilateral official development cooperation, i.e. direct cooperation with a partner country. With its partners, and in consultation with other donor countries, the BMZ elaborates country strategy papers and identifies common priority areas. Country strategy papers are the key management instrument of the BMZ and the basis for medium-term cooperation. The precise arrangements are laid down in agreements, which set out in detail the objectives, time schedules, form and volume of support. This support may take the form of loans on favourable terms, consultancy and training services, the promotion of private sector investment, grants and scholarships, but also emergency aid. The BMZ commissions the German implementing organisations with executing these agreements, and monitors the results of their work.

Cooperation at international level. If we are to resolve global problems, we need to work together closely with international institutions. The Federal Republic of Germany is actively involved in these institutions as part of European and multilateral development cooperation. It is represented on all important bodies, where it puts forward the strategies and positions adopted in German development policy and works to enhance the efficiency of multilateral organisations. And, last but not least, the BMZ manages Germany's contributions at international level, including financial contributions to the European Development Fund, its shares in the World Bank and the regional development banks, and its financial support for the different funds and programmes of the United Nations and the International Monetary Fund (IMF).

Cooperation with non-governmental organisation. In addition to the state-owned development cooperation organisations, a large number of non-governmental organisations, or NGOs, also work in this field. Church organisations, political foundations and other private bodies have long-standing experience, work more closely with poor and underprivileged groups and can mobilise self-help and individual initiative. In addition to providing financial support for the work of these organisations, the BMZ also exchanges views and experiences with them. Equally, NGOs are involved in fomulating the BMZ's country, regional and sector strategies.

Evaluation. Development cooperation can only be regarded as successful if the financial and human resources available are deployed usefully and effectively. For this reason, the BMZ not only regularly reviews the use of budget funds to ensure that they have been used for the intended purpose but also has the development impact of its projects assessed by means of evaluations carried out by external appraisers. The Ministry has a wide range of instruments which it uses to evaluate projects. This helps us to learn from any setbacks encountered and apply approaches that have proved successful to other projects.

Scientific Advisory Council to the Federal Ministry for Economic Cooperation and Development. The Scientific Advisory Council advises the BMZ on all development policy issues. The Council is an independent body, whose members serve on an honorary basis; it produces scientific reports and comments either on behalf of the BMZ or on its own initiative. The Council's statutes stipulate that it may comprise a maximum of 30 academics. New members are proposed by the Council and appointed by the Minister for Economic

Cooperation and Development for a six-year term. Membership can be extended by four years. The Council generally meets three times a year for consultative meetings and, in addition, members form various working groups, in which they draft comments on topical issues. The Council currently consists of 21 experts from fields relevant to development policy. Topics tackled in recent years include state-building and the rule of law, the trade policy of sub-Saharan African countries and supplying drugs for people living with AIDS as a means of poverty alleviation. The pertinent comments of the Council are published in the "BMZ Special" series and are available on the BMZ website.

Development Policy in Parliament. The German Bundestag (Parliament) addresses development policy in various ways. These include debates on the fundamental principles of development policy, debates on topical issues or specific regions and the decisions taken by the Committee on Economic Cooperation and Development (AwZ) or other committees and bodies. The debates are based on reports produced by the federal government, current political events or international conferences. Parliamentary questions and motions on relevant issues are also debated in the Bundestag. Every autumn the draft budget presented by the federal government for the coming year is debated. Since the 14th legislative period (1998 to 2002), policy statements on development have been an integral part of the debates of the Bundestag. Increasingly, development policy concerns are also being taken into consideration in crisis management and prevention, foreign trade and foreign policy[35].

BMZ disposes of certain financial resources intended for the implementation of the relevant programs. It is noteworthy that in the 1990s the Ministry's budget not only did not increase, but was even scaled down in several years (1992, 1996, and 1998). However, the tragic events of September 11, 2001, once again demonstrated the close connection between the security of a separate country and that of the entire world. The German Bundestag therefore adopted a decision to appropriate 0.7% of Germany's GDP for development goals (including combating terrorism, poverty, etc.) on November 16, 2001[36]. An Additional €182 million was appropriated from the 2002 state budget for the struggle against terrorism and regional conflicts. The BMZ budget increased by 4.6% in 2002 in comparison to the previous year and amounted to €3.8 billion or 1.9% of Germany's entire state budget. Approximately 80% of this money was allocated for the development of bilateral cooperation, and 20% – for the development of multilateral cooperation.

What share of this amount is set aside for the African states? Firstly aid is granted under the NEPAD program with a view to halve the poverty scale by 2015. The African states can rely on €90 million under this program. Approximately €100 million are allocated additionally for the development of the countries of the African continent, including the economic development, as well as staff training. Altogether around €200 million, namely somewhat more than 5% of the FMEC budget, have been appropriated for the African trend in 2002[37].

The Ministry's terms of reference also cover stimulating the investment by small and medium-sized German enterprises in developing countries by way of granting long-term credits on preferential terms. Thus, credits can be used both directly for implementing specific projects and for performing pre-investment research. The maximum amount of credit is €1.5 million. Credit is granted at the annual interest of 2.5% for the poorest countries of the world and at 3.5% interest for the rest of the developing countries for the term of up to 15 years, with a maximum grace period of 5 years.

Since the moment of its establishment, BMZ has accorded grants and subsidies for implementing the projects of German Non-Governmental Organizations – churches, political parties funds (around 70 various organizations) in developing countries. It helps to involve wide circles of the German public in implementing aid programs, to establish direct contacts with the neediest strata of population in developing countries, and to deepen the mutual understanding and interosculation of cultures.

An important feature of Germany's manpower policy in implementing the various projects in developing countries is an active involvement of youth in this work. Thus, under the European volunteers' program people aged 18 to 25, with completed vocational training, are granted the opportunity to work for two years under the direction of experienced specialists in developing countries. At the same time, Germany's representatives are protected by a special law on the legal and social plane.

The so-called integrated experts working in developing countries on contract terms and receiving the local salary enjoy similar insurance arrangements. They receive grants and a "traveling allowance" on returning to and finding a job in Germany.

But for all that BMZ itself does not implement any projects or programs in developing countries. Its functions encompass planning the entire activity in the field of cooperation, conducting relevant negotiations with the developing countries, financing the various West-German Non-Governmental Organizations and coordinating their activity in the Third World, coordinating measures with the other donor countries and international agencies, and supervising the use of financial resources.

Direct implementation of BMZ programs and projects is carried out by other organizational structures, among them:

1. The German Development Bank – "Kreditanstalt für Wiederaufbau" (KfW)

2. The German Society for Technical Cooperation – "Deutsche Gesellschaft für Technische Zusammenarbeit GmbH" (GTZ)

3. The German Investment and Development Company – "Deutsche Investitions– und Entwicklungsgesellschaft" (DEG)

4. The Federal Institute for Geosciences and Natural Resources – "Bundesanstalt für Geowissenschaften und Rohstoffe" (BGR)

5. The National metrology institute – "Physikalisch-Technische Bundesanstalt" (PTB)

6. The German Development Service – "Deutscher Entwicklungs dienst" (DED)

7. Capacity Building International – "Internationale Weiterbildung und Entwicklung (InWEnt) GmbH"[38]

The major part of BMZ's financial resources is allocated for financial aid projects. Within the framework of financial aid, funds are allocated for commodities and investments, including the associated expenses on establishing the economic and social infrastructure, as well as directly for industrial branches. The Federal government offers grants and subsidies to development banks in the Third World countries so as to provide the small and medium-sized industrial and agricultural enterprises with credit.

A significant part of Germany's financial aid to developing countries is rendered on behalf of BMZ by the **German Development Bank – "Kreditanstalt für Wiederaufbau" (KfW)**. Its authorized capital reaches €500 million, of which €400 million is the Federal government's contribution, and 100 million is the contribution of the states (Bundesländer). Within the framework of the Federal government's financial aid, the bank makes investments both in branches of goods manufacturing and in the economic and social infrastructure, under the projects proposed by the representatives of the developing countries, including the African ones. The bank's experts are also are widely involved in performing expert judgments of the proposed projects, their recommendations serving as ground for financing on the part of BMZ. The bank frequently operates as a tool of mixed financing, namely uses the funds allocated by the ODA and means from other sources to implement certain projects. Although the general conditions of crediting are thereupon somewhat tougher than under ODA, they are nevertheless more favorable than the market terms.

Africa accounts for a considerable share of the total amount of resources appropriated by the bank to developing countries. Altogether the African continent received 34% of the allocated funds from the Bank in 2002, while the countries of Asia obtained 44%, Latin America – 9%, and Europe (including Turkey) – 13%. The major African recipients of the Bank's resources are Egypt, Morocco, Tunisia, the Sudan, Tanzania, Kenya, and Ghana. The Bank's funds in Africa are distributed as follows: economic infrastructure – 47%, branches of goods manufacturing – 36%, social infrastructure – 15%, other branches – 2%[39].

Technical support from BMZ is provided free of charge. Attention here is concentrated on the financing of West-German counselors and advisers who work with developing countries, on training national experts of every description, including executive personnel, either in the Third World or in Germany, etc.

BMZ renders the major part of technical aid through **the German Society for Technical Cooperation – "Deutsche Gesellschaft für Technische Zusammenarbeit GmbH" (GTZ).**

The German Society for Technical Cooperation was founded in 1975. In 2003 the number of the GTZ employees reached 10,000 people, around 8,500 experts work directly in Germany's 130 partner countries. The company has representations in 63 countries of the world. On the African continent the GTZ is represented in the RSA, Egypt, Morocco, Tunisia, Nigeria, Ethiopia, Tanzania, and the Ivory Coast. The GTZ headquarters are located in Frankfurt. At present the company is carrying out more than 2,700 projects in developing countries, including Africa. It plays an important role in formation of human capital there. Structurally, it consists of 4 departments:

• Africa south of the Sahara
• Asia
• Latin America
• The Mediterranean, Europe, and Central Asia

The company is managed by two directors – Dr. Bernd Eisenblätter and Wolfgang Schmitt.

Under an agreement with the German government the company operates in the so-called "classical" developing countries of Africa, Asia, and Latin America. The choice of partner countries is conducted in accordance with BMZ. Although there is no definite list of partner countries, such international agencies as the United Nations, the World Bank, or the Organization for Economic Co-operation and Development work out certain criteria for priority lines of the GTZ interaction with developing countries, based on the GDP, per capita income, external debt, etc.

While drafting the relevant projects and programs, the GTZ also involves governmental, economic, and public structures of the partner countries, important for human capital formation.

The Company's main goals include planning and implementing technical aid projects and programs, selecting the relevant staff in the Federal Republic to work under them, planning and implementing programs for training and retraining of the national staff of experts for the relevant projects, supplying these projects with equipment as well as financial screening of the draft on funds. The GTZ also supports programs of structural reforms in developing countries, projects of environmental protection, saving tropical forests, water purification, struggle against AIDS, etc.

The company coordinates its actions with other agencies and services, such as the German Development Bank – "Kreditanstalt für Wiederaufbau" (KfW), German Investment and Development company – "Deutsche Investitions– und Entwicklungsgesellschaft" (DEG), German Development Service – "Deutscher Entwicklungsdienst" (DED) and others.

In Egypt, for instance, a joint representation of the company and of the German Bank KfW is established, thus facilitating the coordination of technical and financial cooperation in the North African region[40].

One of the new trends in the company's activity is teamwork with private businessmen under the "Public Private Partnership" (PPP) program. The aim of the program is to consolidate the interests of political institutions and private businessmen, which coincide in many aspects. During the first four years of the program it has implemented around 1,000 projects with 250 companies in 60 countries, including more than 200 projects in Africa.

In 2002, Africa received 46.5% of the GTZ financial resources, allocated to developing countries. The main recipients were Kenya, Somalia, the DRC, Egypt, Mali, etc. The largest part of these funds has been directed to agriculture, health protection, rural development, to the struggle against AIDS, environmental protection (54.8%) as well as to infrastructure (27.6%)[41].

Hereinafter the authors will exemplify the GTZ activity in the African countries and in particular in human capital formation.

In Ethiopia GTZ has been exercising its activities for more than 35 years – since 1972. Among the main lines of GTZ business in this country are:

1. Protection of natural resources and food safety. The GTZ finances actions aimed at increasing the efficiency of the land by means of biological protection of the soil against erosion, using new high-yielding varieties, improving crop rotation, using modern compact equipment, diversifying production in such areas as Oromo, Tigray, and Amhara. The cooperation is of a long-term character, emergency actions are possible in case of drought and other natural calamities.

2. Professional training of the staff. GTZ has participated directly in the drafting of the governmental program of education reform in Ethiopia. Germany renders assistance in training teachers, businessmen, and managers. Actually Germany was the only country constantly helping Ethiopia to implement the education reform.

3. Institutional support. The GTZ provided Ethiopia with direct help in reforming the federal system in the 1990s. German experts also participated in the drafting of a new municipal law, in restructuring communes and administrative centers, in the activity of urban authorities related to improving the municipal economy system, especially in the Amhara and Tigray areas.

The GTZ has worked in the Ivory Coast for over 25 years. At present it is engaged in the following trends of activity:

• Reforestation

• Development of education

• Improvement of the medical care system

• Support of private business

Struggle against trafficking of children and the worst forms of using child labor

Many projects, notably in the country's northern areas, had to be suspended due to the political and economic crisis, which started in this African country in September, 2002.

In Egypt the GTZ primary goals involve:

1. *Aid in building a socially-oriented market economy*. German advisers render assistance in implementing and operating financial and administrative services at the small and medium-sized enterprises in the Arab Republic of Egypt, participate in professional training of the entrepreneurial and administrative staff, establish links between the state and private structures.

2. *Environmental protection and resources*. German experts, along with public services, carry out explanatory work among the population as to the necessity to combat environmental pollution, particularly in urban areas. Close attention is focused on industrial processing of waste, on preserving the vegetative environment, setting up relevant institutes responsible for the population's ecological safety.

3. *Water purification and water-supply*. German scientists have developed new technologies for water purification and water saving, successfully approved in Egypt.

The GTZ activity in the SAR started somewhat later, in 1993, upon the conclusion of the so-called transitional phase and establishment of the new structure of authority in this country. From 1993 to 2000, the GTZ had financed projects amounting altogether to DM 200 million (€391 million), DM 83 million of those (€162 million) were used to support the reform of state structures in the SAR. Only 12 projects were implemented in 1994, whereas in 2000 their number reached 43. The basic lines of the GTZ activity in the SAR encompass:

• Social administration and decentralization
• Development of a system of municipal services and local economy
• Training of qualified personnel
• Programs to develop the economy and employment

Special attention is devoted to eradicating poverty, combating AIDS, to social development, and protection of the richest natural resources[42].

All these examples testify that the GTZ operates actively in various states of the African continent and focuses its activity on the trends most important to the country in question.

Another important tool in organizing cooperation between the private German (mainly average) capital and the developing countries is the German Development Company (DEG), named also the German Financial Company for Investments in Developing Countries – "Deutsche Investions-und Entwicklungsgesellschaft" (DEG), founded in 1961. In essence, DEG is a financial and consulting institute for private direct investments in the Third World, including Africa.

As the DEG emphasizes, "Investments in developing countries are a component of the modern entrepreneurial strategy. Investments in developing countries are investments in our future – in the future of our enterprises"[43].

The DEG's main task consists, therefore, in searching potential partners for German companies, selecting projects, conducting pre-investment surveys, granting subsidies and consultations with a view to minimize the possible risk while allocating investments in the economy of young states.

It is worth mentioning that the DEG becomes a partner for a certain time only, selling its interest upon the expiry thereof and placing the released capital in new enterprises. Thus it repeatedly increases the opportunities to create favorable conditions for German businessmen for their entry into the economy of the developing countries. Already in the late 1970s the total amount of investments in projects with DEG's assistance constituted DM 3.4 billion, i.e. it exceeded the DEG's own authorized capital by a factor of 3.4.

The DEG's main line of business is creation of joint enterprises in developing countries with the participation of local and German private capital. Concurrently, it is emphasized that it is willing to tie up funds in any branches and projects. It accords no branch priorities. The DEG restricts its participation in large-scale companies' projects to a share of 35% in order to encourage the involvement of small German enterprises in developing countries, including the African ones.

It is also noteworthy that the DEG is represented in 50 national and regional banks of the developing countries. Owing to that fact as well as to its close contacts with the banks of western countries and international financial agencies, it is able to render additional financial assistance to German businessmen.

In 2002, the DEG financed projects to the total amount of €463.7 million as compared to €412.0 million in 2001. These means were distributed as follows: €187.7 million (40.5%) were earmarked for Asian states, 102.6 million (22.1%) – for Eastern Europe, 95.1 million (20.5%) – for Latin America, and finally 77.7 million (16.8%) – for Africa. Unfortunately, the share of Africa in DEG's financial investments assigned for developing countries almost halved from 1990 to 2002 – from 42% to 22%[44]. As to the branchwise distribution of funds, 37.7% of DEG's budget was appropriated for the manufacturing industry, 36.2% – for the banking sector, 20.8% – for infrastructure, development, 3.5% – for the agrarian sector, and 2.0% – for the administrative sector[45].

The following paragraphs contain an exemplification of DEG's activity in the African countries throughout the last years.

1. A project to the amount of DM 7.5 million (€14.6 million) for the modernization of the two largest banana plantations in Cameroon with a view to reduce production costs and to increase their competitiveness in the European market. The implementation of this project has brought about the creation of additional 5.5 thousand jobs, 5 small size enterprises for processing agricultural production, the construction of a hospital and a new loading port terminal.

2. An eight-million-euro project for the development of a modern mobile telephone system in Uganda. This African country has the world's lowest rate of telephones installed (30 phones per 1,000 inhabitants) at present. In 1997, the state telephone network disposed of 60,000 numbers only. Due to the implementation of DEG's project 89,000 people in Uganda had become users of the mobile telephone system by 2003. Germany's DEG has actively cooperated in this project with the Ugandan company MNT Holdings Ltd., the Swedish company Telia A.B., and with the South African company Mobil.

3. With DEG's financial and consulting support a German enterprise, Dura Tufting GmbH, created a fellow subsidiary close by Pretoria, Dura Automotive Ltd., which makes carpet covering for

automobiles, including BMW and Mercedes-Benz, using the local cheap labor.

4. The DEG financed the creation of a joint German-Egyptian enterprise ATOS in Egypt, to produce vegetative extracts for Germany's pharmaceutical industry using a wide selection of local Egyptian raw material[46].

In addition to the activities of the abovementioned institutions, a well-adjusted system of information on the state of affairs in the Third World as a whole and in its separate regions, contributes to the expansion of Germany's cooperation with the developing countries. These functions are performed by the German Chamber of Commerce (Aussenhandelskammer – AHK), whose experts work actively in the African states. The chamber was founded in 1901. Now the AHK is represented in 120 countries of the world, it maintains close contacts with 1,400 enterprises. The AHK's primary goals are listed hereinafter:

• collecting and processing the relevant information by countries
• selling and advertising German products
• providing assistance in the management of enterprises in Germany's partner-countries
• consulting the enterprises' management
• lobbying the interests of German businessmen
• sponsoring business negotiations
• searching for business partners abroad
• organizing the process of training in the basics of entrepreneurial activity
• drafting trade and economic agreements
• organizing business conferences and workshops

As far as African countries are concerned, AHK has representations in Algeria, Egypt, Morocco, Libya, the Sudan, Tunisia, and Nigeria. In the SAR there are even 2 representations of AHK – in Johannesburg and in Capetown.

In addition to AHK, the Germany Trade and Invest (GTaI), Chambers of Commerce and Industry (AHKs), banks, Germany's official representations abroad, and special representations of 30 developing countries in Germany (including the Ivory Coast, Gabon, Cameroon, Morocco, Mauritius, Senegal, Somalia, and Tunisia) are also engaged in collecting the relevant information on Africa.

BMZ periodically publishes relevant reference books specifying not only the main activity of departments, institutes, and agencies dealing with the issues of cooperation with the Third World, but also their addresses and phone numbers.

Public organizations, particularly unions and associations on business cooperation, also play an essential part in the expansion of business contacts with the African states.

A public agency, the "Southern Africa Initiative of German Business" (SAFRI), is instrumental in the development of cooperation of German private capital with the countries of the South African region, and in particular with the SAR. SAFRI's constituent assembly took place in Stuttgart, on January 17, 1997, under the chairmanship of Jürgen U. Schrempp – DaimlerChrysler AG's chief executive. Some of Germany's largest organizations participated in the assembly, among them the African association, the Federation of German Industries (Bundesverband der Deutschen Industrie), the German Chambers of Commerce and Industry (Deutscher Industrie– und Handelskammertag) – the latter, together with Germany's government, actually advanced the idea to establish SAFRI already in 1995 – as well as German businessmen having long-term economic contacts with Africa.

SAFRI's main mission is to promote closer cooperation between the German business and the private sector of the countries of South Africa, first of all with the RSA. As SAFRI's chairman, Jürgen Schrempp emphasized, "Investments in the countries of Africa are a component of the modern entrepreneurial strategy. The placement of funds in the African economy is an investment in our future – in the future of our enterprises" [47]. SAFRI's main task consists, therefore, in searching for potential partners for German companies, selecting projects, performing market research, offering consultations with a view to minimize the possible risk while implementing investments in the economy of the countries of the South African region, collecting and structurizing information, and establishing direct contacts between German and South African businessmen and companies.

The employees of SAFRI's central office located in Stuttgart maintain permanent contacts with sponsors and other German associations supporting SAFRI, perform the information interchange with the German chamber of commerce and industry in Johannesburg and with SAFRI's member companies. SAFRI has at its disposal an extensive database on all the countries of the South African region, an extended network of personal contacts throughout Africa, and close contacts with the German business circles as well as with the governments of Germany and of the African states, with the ministries and departments related to the trade and economic cooperation.

According to SAFRI experts, commercial links between Germany and the region of South Africa are extensive, deep, sustained on a long-term basis and quite successful at large. Concurrently, the circle of the German companies maintaining relations with the SAR and other African countries is rather restricted. This phenomenon is explained by the fact that the perceptions of the German businessmen of Africa in general and the SAR in particular are rather scanty. Furthermore, (owing to mass media) for the majority of Germans Africa is associated with backwardness, diseases, wars, conflicts, criminality, corruption at the state level, drought, and other natural cataclysms as well as with poverty. One of SAFRI's main tasks is to give a more realistic picture of modern Africa, to show the prospects of development of interrelations between Germany and the countries of the African continent.

An example of such activity was the arrangement of joint conference of SAFRI and the World Bank in December 1997 in Stuttgart, attended by about 400 German companies as well as governmental and public agencies. Shortly prior to the beginning of the conference the executive secretary of SADC (South African Development Community) had invited the German businessmen to take part in a meeting with African businessmen in Windhoek, capital of Namibia. The meeting resulted in signing the "Windhoek declaration" determining the main goals of the German-South African cooperation and drafting specific measures for the accomplishment of these goals.

An African business forum, convened in June 2000 in Berlin under SAFRI's direct participation, was attended by 700 representatives of the business circles, political and public figures, among them Germany's chancellor, Gerhard Schröder, two German federal ministers and the majority of SADC leaders.

Schröder's participation in this action confirmed Germany's growing interest in Africa including its southern region, and demonstrated state support to the development of German-African business cooperation[48].

Beside large forums, SAFRI organizes business visits of German entrepreneurs to Africa as well as special workshops for South African businessmen in Germany, which are very important for the increase of the local human capital. In particular, 23 German businessmen visited the SAR in 2003, meeting representatives of the local business circles. German businessmen expressed great interest in the increase of cooperation in such areas as tourism, mining industry, and construction.

One of the mainstreams of SAFRI's activity is the preparation of African experts in the commercial sphere. In 2000, SAFRI's experts created a special Human Development Program. Its essence is reduced to the staff training of South African businessmen who undergo special preparation in South Africa, and subsequently in Germany, in the companies maintaining close business ties with Africa. The basic form of training is business-workshops. In the period 2000–2001 alone, 400 South African businessmen received vocational training[49].

In 2002 SAFRI announced a contest for the most efficient small and medium-sized enterprise among the SADC member states. The results of the competition were to be summed up at the end of 2003.

Alongside SAFRI, 17 other associations on business cooperation with the African countries function in Germany. They serve as an important addition to the above-enumerated governmental and business structures, whereas their public nature allows them to manifest greater flexibility in the search for the most efficient solutions, convenient to both German and African business partners.

Briefly recapitulating the foregoing paragraph, the authors of this work arrive at the conclusion that various state, private, and public agencies are established in Germany and function rather successfully, with an objective to enhance cooperation with the African states. From the point of view of fulfillment of the Millennium development goals they play an important role in the human capital formation in the continent. Each of these organizations has its respective structure and fulfils various tasks, but all of them work in close interaction with each other and foster in various forms the development of trade and economic cooperation between Germany and the states of the African continent.

---

[1] Frankfurter Allgemeine. 20.10.1992.

[2] OECD. Efforts and policies of the members of the Development Assistance Committee. Development Cooperation Report. Paris. 1996. P. 15.

[3] Stuttgarter Zeitung. 17.09.2002.

[4] www.aes.org.ru/rus/fact3.htm

[5] Ibidem.

[6] Европейский Союз: Факты и комментарии. Выпуск 8–9 (13–14): апрель-сентябрь 1998 г., Москва, октябрь 1998.

[7] Европейский Союз: Факты и комментарии. Выпуск 1 (15): октябрь-декабрь 1998 г., Москва, январь 1999.

[8] Европейский Союз: Факты и комментарии. Выпуск 2 (16): январь–март 1999 г., Москва, апрель 1999.

[9] www.act.org.de

[10] Frankfurter Allgemeine. 22.03.2000.

[11] http://ec.europa.eu/development/geographical/cotonouintro_en.cfm

[12] Европейский Союз: Факты и комментарии выпуск 1 (22) сентябрь-ноябрь 2000 г. Москва, январь 2001 г.

[13] www.aes.org.ru/rus/fact10.htm; Европейский Союз: Факты и комментарии, выпуск 2 (23) декабрь 2000 – февраль 2001 г. Москва, апрель 2001 г.

[14] www.aes.org.ru/rus/fact12.htm; Европейский Союз: Факты и комментарии, выпуск 3 (24) март 2001 – май 2001 г. Москва, июнь 2001 г.

[15] Berliner Zeitung. 23.04.2002

[16] www.aes.org/rus/fact18.htm Выпуск 31 декабрь 2002 г. – февраль 2003 г. Москва, март 2003 г.

[17] www.aes.org.ru/rus/fact19.htm Европейский Союз: Факты и комментарии Выпуск 32 март 2003 г. – май 2003 г. Москва, июнь 2003

[18] Exportmärkte Deutschlands: Profile und Statistiken zu den 50 wichtigsten Abnehmerländer deutscher Produkte. Köln, 2002. S.16

[19] http://siteresources.worldbank.org/DATASTATISTICS/Resources/GNIPC.pdf

[20] At-Ta'adad al-Amm li-Succan va Iscan. 1996. Cairo, 1998. p. 42–48 (in the Arab language).

[21] http://www.giswatch.org/gisw2008/country/Egypt.html

[22] Middle East and North Africa 2002. UN. 2001. P. 464.

[23] www.presidency.gov.eg/html/information.html

[24] Estimated on the basis of www.presidency.gov.eg. And of «На пороге XXI века». С. 218–219.

[25] www.nua.com

[26] Frankfurter Allgemeine. 17.03.2002.

[27] «Договор об учреждении Европейского Экономического Сообщества», 25 марта 1957 г. See: «Договоры, учреждающие Европейские Сообщества» М., 1994 г. 387 с.

[28] Ibidem (p. 196–198).

[29] See: Treaties establishing the European Communites. V. 1, Luxembourg, 1987, 1118 p.

[30] Ibidem.

[31] Европейский Союз: Факты и комментарии выпуск 2 (19) декабрь 1999 г. – февраль 2000 г. Москва, март 2000 г.

[32] Европейский Союз: Факты и комментарии выпуск 3 (20) март – май 2000 г. Москва, июнь 2000 г.

[33] This part of the monograph was prepared with the financial support of the Russian Foundation for Humanities Project 09-02-00551a / Данный раздел исследования при финансовой поддержке РГНФ в рамках научно-исследовательского проекта РГНФ Роль человеческого капитала в формировании образа страны в многополярном мире: сравнение российских и африканских реалий. 09-02-00551a.

[34] www.bmz.de

[35] http://www.bmz.de/en/ministry/structure/index.html

[36] Entwicklungszusammenarbeit in Zahlen. Bonn, 2003. S. 2.

[37] Ibid. S. 3–5.

[38] www.bmz.de

[39] www.kfw.de

[40] www.gtz.de

[41] Ibidem.

[42] www.gtz.de

[43] www.deginvest.de

[44] www.deginvest.de

[45] Ibidem.

[46] www.deginvest.de

[47] Süddeutsche Zeitung. Stuttgart. 18.01.1997.

[48] Berliner Zeitung. 27.06.2000.

[49] www.safri.com

Chapter 2. NEW TRENDS IN THE MOVEMENT OF GOODS AND LABOR BETWEEN AFRICA AND GERMANY

2.1. Business relations: from raw materials to modern technologies[1]

Development of the world economy is increasingly characterized by interrelated and multi-view processes of globalization and liberalization of economic ties, promoting the accelerated formation of the common market of commodities, services, capitals, and labor. As a consequence, the economy of the majority of countries is becoming increasingly open. Expansion of global economic links occurs faster than general global economic growth; the formation has therefore turned into a major factor of development of the world economy.

In 1988 export growth amounted to 8% or (in the absolute expression) $253 billion, whereas in 2000 it grew to 8.7%, or $6.998 billion. The share of export in the total world GNP increased from 17% in 1988 to 18.4% in 2000. In the African states this figure equaled 22–24%. It was higher than in Latin America and Southern Asia, where it did not exceed 16% of the GNP[2]. However, Africa's high export quota in the GNP rather indicates just the raw material tendency of export than the degree of openness of the region in question, or the level of its involvement in the world economy.

The growing participation of the developing countries has developed into an important feature of international trade; thus their share in world exports amounted to 22.8% in 1990, reached 28.9% in 1996, and increased to 30.1% by 2001. Unfortunately, the foregoing tendency does not apply to the African region, which is characterized by a further decrease in the cumulative world export from 2.3% in 1990 to 1.3% in 2001. African import was in similar situation – its share in the world trade stably declined from 3.6% in 1980 to 1.9% in 2001[3]. Such phenomena in the foreign trade of Africa are regarded by the majority of researchers as a deep crisis. This was exactly the conclusion drawn by the GATT experts estimating the condition of this area in the 1980s. As the above-mentioned statistical data demonstrate, the 1990s are marked by an even greater decrease of the indicators – more than by a factor of 2.5 as compared to 1980.

The crisis condition of African export was a consequence of an adverse conjuncture of a number of raw materials markets where the African countries sell a large share of their goods. The decrease in foreign exchange receipts has finally limited the region's capability to import goods and services.

The condition of the region's foreign trade was also aggravated by a crisis in export strategy implemented under the programs of structural reorganization and adaptation, developed by the International Monetary Fund (IMF) and the World Bank (WB). This strategy, aimed at accelerated export of raw materials and energy carriers, has collided with new tendencies in the world economy. Specifically, it had to deal with the tendency towards reducing the material and power consumption in the production of the developed countries, with the transition from the industrial to the post-industrial pattern of development characterized by growing diversification of hi-tech methods, and integration of modern computer technologies in production process.

The relative exclusion of the African countries from the world market was brought about by the changes in, above all, the commodity composition of the trade exchange in the world economy.

Certain changes, related mainly to the rise in oil prices and in the prices of some types of raw materials, particularly gold, were observed by the beginning of the 21st century in the world raw material market. Under such conditions some African countries stood a chance of somewhat improving their position both due to more favorable world market trends, and by seeking unconventional partners, so as to conclude trade agreements on new conditions. The attention of governments of a number of countries has therefore turned to Germany. This applies primarily to the oil-producing states of the North African region as well as to the African South.

Due to stagnation of the economy and of a number of export branches, Germany was in its turn also interested in seeking new partners in foreign markets, including Africa, in spite of the general tendency towards intensification of European trade.

Germany's position in the system of the world economy is distinguished by a close connection of the German economy with the world market, by the scarcity of its own sources of raw materials, and by the industrial branches' structure, formed under the influence of export-oriented production. More than 50% of Germany's industrial output is sent overseas, 35% of Germany's GDP is created in the export sector. The majority of German companies are export-oriented small and medium-sized businesses, mostly specializing in mechanical engineering. But for German export earnings, the European Union's common trade balance would have been negative[4].

In foreign trade operations the main partners of Germany are the EU countries; they account for more than 70% of Germany's volume of foreign trade[5]. At the same time, the Federal Republic is interested in expanding the geography of the export-import transactions, including the development of links with the African continent, as the majority of countries thereof are resource-rich countries. However, the major obstacle in the way of increasing foreign trade expansion in this direction is the narrowness of the domestic markets of the overwhelming majority of African countries, backwardness of their economy, the low level of industrial development, huge external debts, economic backwardness, and the population's low purchasing parity. Despite an acute need for machines, machine-tools, vehicles, etc. they cannot yet absorb a significant part of the German export, 90% of which consists of manufactured goods. Furthermore, the German monopolies are forced to compete in the African market with both the former metropolitan countries – England and France, and the new partners – the USA, Italy, and China.

Regarding the bilateral trade relations, Africa is primarily a supplier of raw materials for German industry, and a market for German industrial output. An extremely low supply of its own oil and gas production rendered Germany completely dependent on the import of these types of raw material. Despite a number of actions aimed at saving fuel and energy and turning from oil to the use of other energy carriers, the dependence of the German economy on the import of oil and gas supplies is tending to grow in the near future. Africa is one of the important centers for supplying Germany with these types of fuel (along with the Russian Federation, Norway, and Great Britain).

Libya was Germany's main African oil partner from 1980 to 2000. Although the volumes of supplies somewhat dwindled in the 1990s, by the beginning of the new century they were reinstated at the level of 1980, amounting to 14.5 million tons in 1999, i.e. 65% of all the African oil supplies to Germany and covering 13.7% of the country's import demands. According to the Federal Ministry of Economics and Technology (Bundesministerium für Wirtschaft und Technologie, BMWi), the import from Libya dropped to 11.4 million tons in 2000, and to 11 million tons in 2001[6]. Nevertheless, in 2007 Libya was the fourth-largest raw materials supplier for Germany (after Russia, Norway and Great Britain).

Algeria is the second most important source of supply of African oil. This country's oil supplies to Germany made up 4.2 million tons in 1999, or 19.3% of Africa's oil import and 4% of the total German oil import. In 2000 Germany imported 5.5 million tons of oil from Algeria[7].

Oil purchasing in Nigeria diminished abruptly: from 11 million tons in 1980 to 1.2 million tons in 1999. Nonetheless, there was a marked increase of Nigeria's import to 1.9 million tons in 2000. Germany's other African oil suppliers – Angola, Gabon, the Republic of the Congo, and Tunisia – account for shares of percent of the total oil import to Germany.

As to gas supplies, Germany's dependence on external sources of this kind of fuel accounts for 78%. Russia will obviously maintain its position as Germany's leading gas supplier in the next decade. However, Germany has concluded long-term contracts on supply of this kind of raw material with Algeria, Libya, and Egypt.

Besides the African oil, which covered more than one third of Germany's demand in certain years, the countries of Africa provide a significant share in supplies of cobalt (the main suppliers – the Democratic Republic of Congo, DRC (former Zaire) and Zambia), bauxites (Guinea), copper (Zambia, the DRC), phosphates (Morocco, Senegal, and Togo), iron ore (Liberia, Mauritania), cocoa-beans (the Ivory Coast, Cameroon, Nigeria, and Ghana), sisal (Madagascar, Tanzania, and Kenya), pyrethrum extract (Kenya), coffee (Kenya, Tanzania, Cameroon, and the Ivory Coast), cotton (Egypt, the Sudan, Mali, Chad, and Uganda) as well as quinine (Zaire, Kenya, and Rwanda) and tropical timber (the Ivory Coast, Ghana, Liberia, Cameroon, and Gabon).

The SAR plays a pivotal role as a supplier of raw materials of strategic importance for Germany, which imports uranium, vanadium, manganese ore, rough diamonds, chrome, platinum, nickel, etc. from the region.

The growing demands of the dynamically developing German economy promoted the growth of the volumes of Germany's trade with the African countries in the 1970s.

Table 1

Volume of Germany's trade turnover with Africa

Year	Volume of export to Africa (mln $)	Africa's share of overall Germany's export (%)	Volume of import from Africa (mln $)	Africa's share of overall Germany's import (%)
1980	7 907	4.1	12 784	6.8
1990	6 957	1.7	8 315	2.4
1995	7 128	1.4	7 545	1.7
2000	6 037	1.1	8 004	1.6
2001	6 843	1.2	6 896	1.4
2006	22 543 (€16 617)	1.86	22 702 (€16 734)	2.27
2007	23 843 (€17 575)	1.82	22 326 (€16 457)	2.13
2008	26 726 (€19 700)	1.98	27 909 (€20 572)	2.52

Estimated on the basis of: UNCTAD Report 2002, pp. 58–75; Deutsche Bundesbank Zahlungsbilanzstatistik vom 10.3.2009.

However, Germany's foreign trade turnover with Africa had declined since the second half of the 1980s – from $20 691 million in 1980 to $15 272 million in 1990, and to $13 739 million in 2001. Whereas in 1980 the share of the states of the African continent in Germany's export and import totaled 4.1% and 6.8% respectively, in 1990 they made up 1.7% and 2.4%, and in 2001 – 1.2% and 1.4% respectively. The general tendency to decrease the German trade turnover with Africa is related both to the common geographical reorientation of the world, flows of commodities in the globalization epoch, to the fall in raw material prices on the world market, and to the extremely unstable dynamics of the oil prices.

Deliveries of finished products from the countries of Africa to Germany are extremely insignificant (less than 1% of German import) and are actually limited to the North African states and the SAR. Basically these are semi-finished goods, fabrics, finished textile articles, foodstuffs, etc.

German exports to the countries of Africa, as well as imports, are accounted for by the oil-producing countries and the SAR, which dispose of a relatively capacious home market of finished products. German leading exports to the African continent are machinery, equipment, and other finished products. Three quarters of Germany's total export to Northern and Tropical Africa and 85% – to the SAR are provided by the seven leading branches of German industry – machinery construction, chemical, steelmaking, automobile, shipbuilding, electrical, and textile industry.

Overall, despite the rather modest role of Africa in Germany's foreign trade turnover, one should not underestimate its significance for the economy of the largest European country. Not only does the African continent provide a considerable share of Germany's demands for raw material, it also represents a perspective market for the leading, largely export-orientated branches of German industry. Furthermore, following the discovery of new, on the assumption of some experts, huge oil and gas fields along the African fault, Africa can become an important sphere of application for German capital in the next decades.

At the same time, a well defined differentiation of interests of German capital in Africa is perceived.

The Table 2 below shows Germany's 10 major export and 10 featuring import partners in Africa.

Table 2

Germany's major trade partners in Africa (2008)[8]

	Import from...	Import value (mln €)	Export to...	Export value (mln €)
1	Libya	5 518,7	SAR	7 300,0
2	SAR	5 299,7	Egypt	2 725,1
3	Nigeria	1 793,4	Algeria	1 490,7
4	Algeria	1 735,2	Morocco	1 478,6
5	Tunisia	1 337,1	Tunisia	1 370,8
6	Egypt	1 168,9	Nigeria	1 246,7
7	Morocco	533,4	Libya	1 047,3
8	Angola	468,6	Angola	402,8
9	Mauritania	135,7	Kenya	232,3
10	Kenya	124,1	Sudan	226,6

Lybia and the SAR rank first in this list, providing almost one third of the overall African turnover with Germany. Regarding the SAR, in 2008 Germany imported goods from this country to the sum of €5.3 billion, equaling nearly 40% of all the German import from the countries of the African continent.

In 2001, Germany had a positive balance in its trade with the SAR, equal to $529.9 million. In 2007 the positive balance maintained and amounted to €2.72 billion ($3.69 billion).

Germany's import from the SAR is dominated by machinery (20,2%). Non-ferrous metals and raw materials also remain South Africa's major exports to Germany (18,6% and 18,1% respectively). The share of ores and metals (7,3%), as well as of food (5,3%) and automobiles (4,7%) in the South African export to Germany, is also quite significant.

85

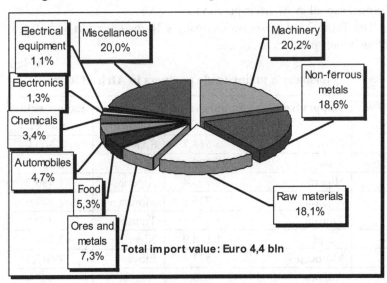

Despite South Africa's modest place in the German foreign trade turnover (27th as the exporter and 29th as the importer), this country will definitely keep its leadership role in Germany's economic relations with the countries of Africa in the near future. Not only does the SAR satisfy Germany's demands for strategically important raw material, but it also represents a capacious and dynamically developing market for many branches of the German industry focused on export.

The North African sub-region has become another important trading partner of Germany, accounting for almost half of Germany's import from the African continent.

The leadership there belongs to Libya, which exports oil and gas to Germany. Oil supplies from this country increased from 4.050 thousand tons in 2002 to 4.118 thousand tons in 2003, or by 1.6%. The German market of hydrocarbonic raw materials is a priority for Libya, as it accounts for about a quarter of the total Libyan export. In the last 2–3 years the growth of oil import from Algeria also became quite significant, Algeria ranking 7th in the list of Germany's suppliers. The import of oil from this North African country to Germany increased from 1.767 thousand tons in 2002 to 2.176 thousand tons in 2003, or by a factor of 1.23. Tunisia also exports oil to Germany; however, its supplies decreased from 217 thousand tons in 2002 to 170 thousand tons in 2003. Concurrently, Germany started bringing in oil from Egypt in 2003; the import from this country made up 170 thousand tons.

Besides hydrocarbonic raw materials, Germany imports products of light and food industry, semi-finished goods, chemicals, some other types of raw materials, electronics, steel, and cast iron from the countries of North Africa.

Thus, for example, the Federal Republic imports from Egypt (besides oil and gas) cotton knitted wear to the amount of €46 million (17% of the total Egyptian export to Germany), aircraft to the amount of €22 million (10% of the Egyptian export), hardware (€17 million, 7.4%), semi-finished goods (€13 million, 5.6%), vegetables (€11.5 million, 5%), clothes and other cotton products (€20.5 million, 9.3%). Germany imports coke from Egypt to the amount of €7.8 million.

Table 3

Structure of the German import from Egypt

Rank	Description of goods	Cost in million Euro
1	Cotton knitted wear	46.1
2	Oil derivatives and natural gas	25.8
3	Aircraft	22.4
4	Hardware	16.8
5	Semifinished goods	12.6
6	Other components	12.5
7	Vegetables	11.4
8	Cottons	11.2
9	Cotton yarn	9.8
10	Coke	7.8

Source: Exportmärkte Deutschlands. p. 59.

As for Tunisia, which occupies the fifth place in the list of African exporter countries (2007 – €1,072 billion), the structure of Germany's import from this North African state differs markedly from the common structure of German import from the countries of Africa. Textile and clothes prevail in the structure of the Tunisian export to Germany (34.7% and 34.2% respectively). The share of oil export in the export structure amounted to 13.0% in 2007. Fig. 2 represents the structure of Tunisian export to Germany.

Fig. 2. **Structure of the German import from Tunisia (2007)**[10]

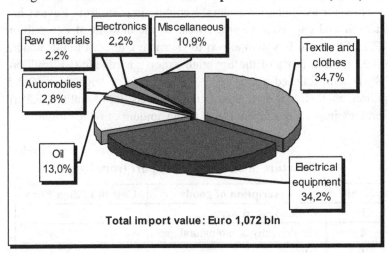

As regards the Ivory Coast, Germany purchases there mainly coffee (Robusta variety) and cocoa, which represent 89% of the total import of this African country to Germany (Wirtschaftstrends Westafrika 2000/2001. BAHI., Köln, 2001. p. 53). Nigeria was a long-established supplier of oil to the German market of hydrocarbonic raw material. However, during the last 5 years Germany's import of oil from Nigeria has been constantly decreasing, on account of re-orientation to other sources. Among Germany's new African suppliers of oil one could single out (besides the already mentioned

Egypt) Angola (918 thousand tons in 2002), Gabon (57 thousand tons in 2003), and Cameroon (51 thousand tons in 2002)[11]. From Zimbabwe Germany imports primarily tobacco, gold, and ferroalloys, whereas from the Republic of the Congo it brings in coffee and cocoa, like from the Ivory Coast.

As to Germany's export, 95% of it is accounted for by the 10 African states enumerated in the following table.

Table 4
Major African importers of German goods (2008)[12]

Country	Import value (mln Euro)
SAR	7 300,0
Egypt	2 725,1
Algeria	1 490,7
Morocco	1 478,6
Tunisia	1 370,8
Nigeria	1 246,7
Libya	1 047,3
Angola	402,8
Kenya	232,3
Sudan	226,6

The main importer of goods from Germany in Africa is the South African Republic (€7 300 mln). The SAR belongs to Germany's 50 major trade partners and occupies the 29th place in the list of world importers of German goods, outstripping such countries as Mexico, Australia and Ukraine. In 2007 Germany registered a positive balance in trade with the SAR, amounting to €2.72 billion.

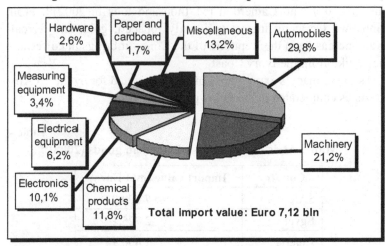

Fig. 3. **Structure of the German export to the SAR**[13]

In the figure:
- Hardware 2,6%
- Paper and cardboard 1,7%
- Miscellaneous 13,2%
- Automobiles 29,8%
- Measuring equipment 3,4%
- Electrical equipment 6,2%
- Machinery 21,2%
- Electronics 10,1%
- Chemical products 11,8%
- Total import value: Euro 7,12 bln

As Fig. 3 demonstrates, the major share of German export to the SAR consists of automobiles (29,8%). Machinery, chemical products and electronics are also among the main export goods, delivered by the Federal Republic to the SAR.

Egypt ranks second after the SAR among the African countries importing German products. The import to the Arab Republic of Egypt from Germany registered €2 725,1 million in 2007. By this indicator, Egypt ranks 44th among the Federal Republic's importers.

Electrical equipment accounts for 20,7% of German supplies to Tunisia. Machinery and textile also represent a significant part of the German export to this North African country (11,8% and 10,7% respectively).

The major ten countries importing the German products also include Angola, Kenya and Sudan, which trade in equipment, automobiles as well as products of electrical industry from Germany.

Fig. 4. **German Export to Egypt (2007)**[14]

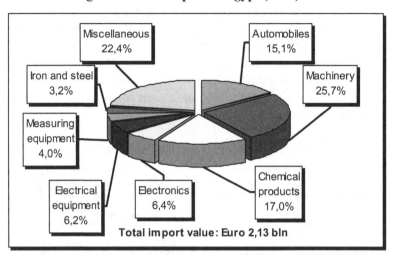

Trade in agricultural commodities for several decades has been one of the most problematic spheres of international trade, significant both to the African and to the developing countries altogether. Despite a liberalization of world trade which emerged after the General Agreement on Tariffs and Trade came into effect in 1948, the agricultural trade sector, because of the dexterous policies of the world's leading powers remained outside this process for many years. Protectionism and subsidizing of trade in agricultural commodities brought about an aggravation of the international trade relations between the two groups of states in the late 1980s – the EU countries having a traditionally high degree of state support for the production of and trade in agricultural commodities, and the US with the other leading manufacturers and exporters of this type of products. Following a compromise between these groups the "Uruguay Round" of the multilateral trade negotiations on agriculture led to an Agreement based on the norms and rules regulating the trade and economic policies of the member states in three areas: access of agricultural commodities to the market, internal budgetary support for the manufacturers, and subsidizing the export of agricultural production[15]. Additionaly, by the end of the round the WTO member nations negotiated a number of obligations on immediate liberalization of trade in agricultural commodities; they also laid down individual commitments in the lists of concessions, which are an appendix to the final act of the "Uruguay Round". Concerning the developing countries, the Agreement stipulates a "smaller volume of commitments, whereas the least developed countries are exonerated completely from them".

Fig. 5. **Germany's Export to Tunisia (2007)**[16]

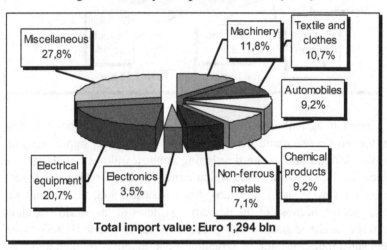

The Agreement is aimed at stimulating the transition of the governments of the WTO member nations from the supporting measures "distorting" trade to the "non-distorting" ones. The pivotal provision regarding the access of agricultural commodities to the market is the commitment to implement the "tariffication", i.e. to convert all the non-tariff import regulatory measures (quotas, licenses, measures to support public enterprises, etc.) to customs tariffs by the proposed recalculation formulas and "tying" the rates of import tariffs for agricultural commodities, i.e. the commitment not to increase them over a certain level, including the duties established in the result of "tariffication". According to the Agreement, the countries undertook to reduce consistently the tariffs established in the process of "tariffication" as well as the tariffs previously in force. A reduction of tariff rates at an average of 36% for industrial countries and 24% for developing countries was to be achieved for the first group over six years after the Agreement came into effect and over 10 years – for the second group. The agreement contained a number of special provisions granting the countries which implement the "tariffication" a right to employ special measures so as to protect their market under certain conditions. The Agreement also stipulated a list of subsidies to be reduced during the transitional period, and from then on subsidizing the export of goods not subject to that operation in the basic period (the end of the 1980s) was to be banned. The Agreement provided for some grants, the application of which was not expressly forbidden, in regard to them the WTO member nations undertook to reduce gradually the volume of subsidized export and the amount of budgetary appropriations under this title. A preferential 10-year transitional period was stipulated for the developing countries, the reduction of export subsidies represented 24% in value terms, and 14% in natural terms[17].

Overall, according to many experts, despite a certain progress in liberalizing the international trade in agricultural commodities registered at the "Uruguay Round", numerous problems in this area remain unsolved.

Thus, the "tariffication" has not brought about a substantial improvement of access to the markets in many sectors of agricultural trade. Though the WTO countries had assumed and fulfilled commitments regarding the access of agricultural commodities to the market, the markets of several commodity groups still remain in part closed. The agreement has also not removed the subsidizing of agricultural export, even at the end of the transitional period many developed countries still employ it on significant scales.

Thus, the liberalization of the area under consideration entails significant difficulties and country contradictions, its essential tasks have not been completely achieved: the continuing subsidies of agricultural export, on-going prohibitive import tariffs for agricultural commodities; the manner of applying tariff quotas as well as an excessively high, according to some WTO member nations, level of governmental support for domestic manufacturers.

In addition to a certain decrease of agrarian protectionism, a spontaneous growth in world prices for some types of agricultural commodities, conditioned by the reduction of export subsidies and of budgetary support for the manufacturers, was one of the consequences of implementation of the agreement. According to tentative estimates by the IMF and the IBRD, the increase in world prices for the formerly subsidized goods were to be from 4% to 10% by 2003: the expected consumer benefits in this case are rather uncertain.

In a brief summary to the given section of the paper the authors arrive at the following conclusions:

1. The share of African states in the Germany's foreign trade decreased in the 1990s of the last century and in the beginning of the 21st century due to both the amplification of intra-regional trade within the European Union and to the instability of raw material and fuel markets, where African countries are present for the most part.

2. Although Germany maintains trade relations practically with all the countries of Africa, the SAR and the countries of the North African region hold priority positions in this area, accounting for more than 80% of total German export and import. This is determined both by a higher level of socio-economic development of these states and by a number of historical, political, and geographical factors.

3. As to the structure of German-African trade, Germany's major exports to the African continent are hi-tech equipment, automobiles, machine-building, and electrical products, whereas the import basically consists of fuel, mineral and agricultural raw material, and semi-finished goods. The SAR, as well as Tunisia, Egypt, Morocco, and Libya represent the only exception, supplying several types of finished products to Germany.

4. In foreign trade with the countries of Africa, Germany is exceeded by its EU partners – France, Great Britain, and Italy. Nevertheless, Germany has occupied increasingly stronger positions in the markets of a number of African states in the last years, successfully

competing with their traditional partners. According to our estimations, in the forthcoming 10 years the volumes of trade of the FRG with the countries of Africa shall grow, this refers notably to the North African states and the SAR.

2.2. Export of labor resources from Africa to Germany[18]

Growth of geographical mobility of labor has become one of the major consequences of globalization. Huge numbers of people change their place of dwelling, the type of settlement, the line of business, the nature of concepts and habits formed over the centuries in rather short time intervals and find themselves in a new, unusual environment, among people who have a completely different way of life, a different system of secular and religious values, and speak a different language.

The problem of coexistence of immigrants and of the local population has been especially acute in Europe in the last 20 years. On the one hand, a stable inflow of foreign workers is necessary for the West-European states to sustain economic growth, compensate for the low level of birth rate and the process of "ageing" of the population of Europe as well as to fill in the less respected, "dirty" jobs which many Europeans do not want to take on. On the other hand, migration entails an aggravation of the socio-political situation in the host country, since the foreign minorities in time become so numerous as to challenge the domination of the native population.

Mass external migrations have become an important characteristic feature of labor forces of the Arab nations of Africa, whereas their influence on the economic and social development of these states has appreciably amplified in the last decades.

The industrial states of the Western Europe and America were traditionally (until the beginning of the 1970s) attractive for people from Arab countries. The gap in the standard of living between the former and the latter was 20–30-fold on average.

A new migration trend emerged in the 1970s and 1980s – the natives of Egypt, Morocco, Tunisia and other countries rushed to the oil-rich countries of the Persian Gulf (Saudi Arabia, Iraq, Kuwait, the

United Arab Emirates, Qatar, and Bahrain) and North Africa (Libya, and to a lesser degree Algeria). Besides the material factor, work in the oil-rich Arab states gave the Arab immigrants a number of advantages in comparison to their position in the European states. In the states of the Gulf there were no language and religious barriers, the way of life in the recipient countries practically did not differ from the lifestyle in the donor countries. Furthermore, in Europe the Arab immigrants were hired for heavy unskilled work rejected by the local population, while in the Gulf countries the natives of the Arab donor countries worked not only in the spheres traditional for immigrants, such as construction, oil extracting, and agriculture, they also quite frequently occupied the prestigious posts of engineers, teachers, managers, etc. This was especially typical of Egyptians, Lebanese, and Palestinians.

By the mid-1980s the share of Arab immigrants in the countries of the Persian Gulf and Libya exceeded 80% of the total migration flow[19].

However, by the beginning of the 1990s the direction of migration flow from the countries of the Arab East and Africa had undergone changes again. Firstly, they were triggered by the Iraqi-Kuwaiti conflict, when following "Operation Desert Storm" more than 1 million Arab immigrants left Iraq due to the aggravation of the economic situation in the country. There was a sharp fall in oil prices that compelled governments of the Persian Gulf countries to prefer much cheaper labor from Southern and Southeast Asia to the Arab experts. Under these circumstances Western Europe regained its attractiveness to immigrants from the Arab countries.

England and, particularly France were traditionally attractive for Africans, drawing numerous immigrants from the former English and French colonies. Germany failed to compete in this respect with its partners from the European Union; however, in some aspects it was a more acceptable country to inhabit for Arab immigrants not only for economic reasons (as Germany is Europe's richest and most dynamically developing country), but also for social-psychological reasons. The Arab countries were never German colonies; the relation of Arabs towards Germans was therefore historically more loyal in comparison to the feelings aroused in them by the former English and French colonizers.

A short digression should be made about the history of Arab migration to Germany. The first Arabs (in this case not separate representatives of this nation, but more or less numerous groups) appeared in German territories at the end of the 18th century in the structure of the Prussian regiments. Some of them got German wives, stayed in Germany and gradually assimilated.

In the 19th and in early 20th century Arabs from Egypt, Iraq, Palestine, and Lebanon came to Germany both in search for work and with the purpose to receive education. They came mainly from rather well-to-do families. By the beginning of World War II their number reached 15–20 thousand by different estimates[20].

During World War II many immigrants from the Arab nations, notably from Egypt and Iraq, which had broken off their diplomatic relations with Hitlerite Germany, were interned on Hitler's orders[21]. However, afterwards, following the establishment of the so-called African corps, Hitler decided to use the Arab immigrants in Germany for propaganda purposes. Basically they were former students and workers from occupied France as well as refugees from Syria and Lebanon, who had left their countries after the introduction of the English troops there. Arabs agreed to cooperate with fascist Germany entertaining the illusion that the Germans would support them in their struggle for liberation from the colonial powers of England and France.

During the war Arabs mostly worked as announcers with the German radio in the Arab language, journalists and even as scouts.

After Germany had lost the war and embarked on a path of cooperation with the Anti-hitlerite coalition states, it needed to restore its destroyed economy under conditions of acute labor shortage caused by appreciable losses of the able-bodied male population. During that period Germany adopted a law on immigrants, facilitating and encouraging the inflow of foreign workers. Already in the 1950s the German industry employed plenty of natives from the East, mainly Turks, but also Arabs.

Thus, in the post-war period the economic motivation of Arab migration to Germany almost completely replaced the political one. Over the next years the political, economic, and social factors of migration acted together, the degree of their importance varied only depending on the development of situation both in Germany and in the Arab donor countries. Migration for military-political motives was most intensive in the late 1960s – early 1970s due to the Arab-Israeli war of 1967 and to the occupation of the Arab territories. The next numerous group of political immigrants arrived in Germany in the mid-1980s following the beginning of the civil war in Lebanon. Another migration upsurge occurred in the early 1990s after the previously mentioned Persian Gulf War. And, finally, in 2002, following the aggravation of relations between the Palestinians and the Israelis, which entailed military actions and civilian casualties on both sides, refugees from Palestine and its neighboring territories rushed again to Germany.

Despite the importance of the political reasons of migration, the socio-economic aspect was the major factor stimulating the migration of people from the South and East to the North and West. The German economy is considered to be the most powerful and stable economy of Europe; the standard of living in Germany is much higher not only in comparison to a number of Arab states, but also to other European countries. Thus, the average per capita income in the beginning of the new millennium amounted in Germany to $26 thousand annually, in Great Britain – to $21 thousand, in France – to $25 thousand, in Italy – $20 thousand, and in Spain – to only $14 thousand annually. Simultaneously the corresponding indicator did not exceed $1 300 per year in the Arab Republic of Egypt, $1 250 in Morocco, $2 050 in Tunisia, $450 in The Sudan, and $1 100 in Syria[22]. The average wages in Germany constitute approximately $1 200 a month, while the average earnings of an Egyptian in the public sector of economy do not exceed $100 to $150, and in the private sector – $300 to $350 a month.

While the difference in the standard of living between Germany and some African states is a powerful factor "attracting" immigrants, then the "pushing out" factors traditionally are unemployment, poverty, and land shortage. Thus, for example, in Egypt, despite certain considerable success in implementing economic reforms, the social costs of the process were rather high.

The rate of unemployment in Egypt reached 8,8 percent in the fourth quarter of 2008 from 9,1 percent a year earlier[23]. However, the unemployment problem in the Arab states is going to aggravate all the more in the near future, as the average annual rates of growth of the labor forces are much higher there than in Europe. Thus, in Germany at the end of the 1990s due to the general low birth rates, which registered only 0.5% annually, the average annual growth of labor forces declined from 0.9% in the 1980s to 0.4% in the 1990s. Meanwhile, the majority of Arab states were distinguished both by high birth rates (Algeria – 2.6%, Egypt – 2.3%, Jordan – 5.4%, Lebanon – 2.1%, Morocco – 2.1%, and Tunisia – 2.0% annually) and by accelerated rates of growth of labor forces, amounting at the beginning of the new century to 5% in Algeria, 3% – in Egypt, 6.2% – in Jordan, 3.4% in Lebanon, 2.8% in Morocco, and 3.5% in Tunisia[24].

It seems obvious that in the next 20–30 years the world demographic situation will develop in such a way that an essential increase in population is likely to occur in the developing countries, while the share of the population of Europe and the US shall constantly decrease. Thus, if approximately 50% of the population of the countries of Africa and Asia are represented by people under the age of 30, the European population is an "old" population, of which a big share of people in the retirement age is typical. Under these conditions the migration of labor forces from the developing countries, including the Arab nations, remains a necessary condition for the existence of the European and in particular German economy. Simultaneously, the authorities of the Arab states are also interested in the outflow of the labor "surpluses" to other states, which is laid down in the extraordinarily liberal emigration legislation in a number of countries of Africa and the Arab East, openly encouraging emigration. Furthermore, the migrant labor transfers serve as one of the basic sources of foreign-exchange revenues for the donor countries. One should also remember that by using foreign labor, Germany, on the one hand, saves on the labor costs (since the wages of a foreign worker are on average 30% lower than the ones of a German) and solves the problem of the so-called "non-prestigious" jobs, which the local population is not eager to take, on the other.

Table 5

Distribution by activity types of the German and foreign laborers and white-collar workers (in %)

Activity Types		Foreigners		Germans	
		1984	2000	1984	2000
1	Laborers	22	14	5	4
2	Skilled workers	36	38	12	10
3	Highly skilled workers and masters	18	20	17	20
4	White-collar workers	14	24	42	50
5	Self-employed	7	3	14	10
6	Officials	2	1	10	6

Source: Rheinisch-Westfälisches Institut für Wirtschaftsforschung. 2001, p. 51.

As Table 5 demonstrates, every second foreigner in Germany (58% in 1984 and 52% in 2000) belongs to the category of skilled workers and laborers, while only one in seven Germans (14% in 2000) can be attributed to this group. White-collar workers are every second German and just one in four foreigners. Alone in the category of highly skilled workers and foremen, foreigners and Germans occupy equal positions – 20% each.

As regards such categories as self-employed and officials, here the biggest gap is observed, which, furthermore, tends to increase: in 1984 there were 2.7 times more German officials and proprietors of their own enterprises than foreigners, while in 2000 the gap was already fourfold.

Thus, to the foreigners' share fall those very types of work which are not popular with the local population. As a rule, it is "dirty", unskilled labor, or work demanding great physical and mental input as well as monotonous work, for example, at the conveyor belt. As to the so-called "prestigious" types of work, this sphere of human activity is reliably protected by German legislation, according to which a significant number of diplomas received outside Germany, the US, and some large European countries, are simply not recognized. Contenders are subjected to a series of professional propriety tests, where they are confronted particularly with the language barrier, a disloyal attitude of the examiners, a specific form of interrogation, etc.

The authors of these lines personally communicated with a dentist from Saudi Arabia, Mr. A. He had studied at German language courses at the Goethe Institute for 8 months (the curriculum in 1993 cost DM8 thousand). Then he completed 12 months of practice with the German Dr. X. in Munich practically free of charge, but despite that, the patients by the end of the term preferred the Arab expert as it was cheaper and the high level of quality was preserved. Furthermore, Mr. A. was extraordinarily gentle and tolerant with his patients. Then he took a seven-stage examination, but, unfortunately, failed to reply to one question on the general theory of medicine, which did not refer directly to his speciality. He therefore failed the examination and was offered to repeat the attempt in a year. Undoubtedly, the medical profession is a special case. However, a similar situation is also observed in other branches, which are attractive to the German population, and whose interests are firmly protected by the German legislation.

The migration flow from Africa to the Federal Republic has been (on the whole, but not by country) decreasing steadily since 1991 (Table 6). The share of Africans in the total amount of immigrants in Germany made up 3,7% in 2007 (3,9% in 2006).

Table 6

Immigration flow from Africa to Germany 1991–2007[25]

Land of origin	1991	1994	1997	2000	2003	2006	2007
Africa total	52 761	38 113	36 767	35 029	35 951	25 585	25 056
Egypt	3 500	2 104	2 264	2 108	1 890	2 091	2 502

Land of origin	1991	1994	1997	2000	2003	2006	2007
Algeria	1 930	4 302	2 766	2 670	2 440	1 348	1 392
Morocco	6 094	3 997	4 142	5 545	6 021	3 797	3 418
Tunisia	2 905	2 539	2 116	2 663	2 579	2 521	2 179

Let us dwell now in more detail on the specific characteristics of the process of migration from the Arab nations to Germany.

Table 7

National structure of immigrants in Germany
(December 31, 2001)

Nationality	Number	%
1. Turks	1,947,938	26.3
2. Yugoslavs	1,085,765	14.7
3. Italians	616,282	8.3
4. Greeks	362,708	4.9
5. Poles	310,432	4.2
6. Arabs	288,115	3.9
7. Austrians	188,975	2.5
8. Portuguese	132,625	1.8
9. Spaniards	128,713	1.7
10. Americans (US)	113,623	1.5
11. Iranians	107,927	1.4
12. Vietnamese	84,138	1.1
Other	2,030,788	27.5
Total	7,398,036	100

Source: Ausländer in Deutschland. No. 2, 2002, p. 8.

As Table 7 shows, at the moment Arabs represent the sixth largest group of immigrants in Germany, considerably behind Turks and Yugoslavs and approaching Greeks and Poles. The general percentage of the Arab immigrants is insignificant – it varies within the limits of 4%. In many respects this is due to a strong penetration of the foreign labor market in Germany by Turks and Yugoslavs, who have been mastering it since the 1950s and 1960s, as well as due to a traditional trend of the main migration streams from the Arab nations to France and, to a lesser degree, to Great Britain. The complexity of the necessary paper work, multi-stage decision-making at obtaining or extending visas as well as a "stricter", as compared to France, immigration legislation are the essential factors hampering the arrival of the Arab immigrants in Germany.

Nevertheless, the Arab immigrants increasingly actively master new territories, the fact that has become especially evident in the 1990s of the last century. Alone in the period between 1991 and 2001, the number of Arab immigrants in Germany tripled[26].

As to the distribution of the Arab immigrants by donor countries, this data is indicated in the following table.

Table 8

**Quantity of the basic groups of immigrants from
the Arab countries on 01.01.2001**

Donor country	Quantity	%
Morocco	81,450	28
Lebanon	54,000	19
Iraq	51,000	18
Syria	24,000	8
Tunisia	24,000	8
Algeria	17,000	6
Egypt	14,000	5
Jordan	11,000	4
The Sudan	4,697	1.6
Libya	2,643	0.8
Yemen	1,586	0.6
Saudi Arabia	738	0.3
The United Arab Emirates	727	0.3
Qatar	89	–
Bahrain	43	–

Source: Ausländer in Deutschland. No. 2, 2001, p. 8.

As Table 8 testifies, the most numerous group of immigrants are Moroccans. Altogether 47.4% of all the Arab immigrants in Germany in 2001 were North Africans. A rather numerous group is formed by Lebanon and Syria (27%) as well as Iraq (19%) – countries involved in various military-political conflicts. Immigrants from the rich countries of the Persian Gulf are the least numerous: by the beginning of the new century they were only 1 597, or approximately 1.5% of all the Arabs living in Germany at that time.

However, it is necessary to make a reservation that this data does not include numerous refugees, in particular Palestinians as well as illegal immigrants living in Germany outside the law. According to some experts, their number varies between 50 and 100 thousand people[27].

All the Arab immigrants in Germany are divided into 3 basic categories:

1. Labor immigrants, i.e. Arabs who have arrived in Germany in search for work. Initially they come without their families, and only after finding a job decide whether to leave their family in the homeland, supporting its well-being by remittances, or to bring their wives and children to Germany. For the most part this is determined by their earnings, nature of work, by the residence place and conditions, interrelations with the locals as well as by the desire and a possibility to obtain a residence permit in Germany.

2. Students who receive education in Germany. As a rule, they are the children of the well-off parents, frequently proprietors of large and medium-sized companies, interested in the good educational level of the heirs. Though the training in Germany is free, considerable expenses are incurred in connection with lodging and food. A small group of Arab students consists of the most gifted young people who have obtained grants in Germany.

3. Refugees and immigrants who have arrived in Germany in search for political asylum as well as from the military conflict zones. It is a special category of immigrants in terms of both its position in German society, and its way of life.

Moroccans represent the most numerous group of immigrants from the Arab countries – they account for 30% of all the registered Arabs living in Germany. They often live in communities in one street or in one area. The majority of Moroccan immigrants are employed in the mineral industry as well as in the chemical and textile industry. Two German states – North Rhine-Westphalia (Nordrhein-Westfalen) and Hessen (the so-called industrial region of Ruhr) host 85% of all the Moroccans. About half of the immigrants from Morocco live in 10 large German cities: in Frankfurt their number reaches 9 500 people, in Düsseldorf – 6 000 people, in Dortmund – 3 300 people, in Cologne – 2 300 people, in Aachen, Bochum, Essen, Krefeld, and Rüsselheim – approximately 1 500 people each. It is noteworthy that the majority of the Moroccan immigrants in Germany are not native Arabs, but Berber-peasants from the Rif mountain areas[28].

Tunisians appeared in Germany by the beginning of the 20th century. At that time 2 000 natives of Tunisia lived on the German ground. However, the migration of Tunisians to Germany on a constant basis began only after 1965, following the adoption of tough anti-immigration laws by the neighboring France. Germany was entering a stage of stable industrial growth in the period in question and needed additional labor, including foreign labor. At present Tunisians are settled throughout Germany. They undoubtedly belong to the elite among the Arab immigrants as they are well educated and work in the manufacturing industry, in the sphere of education, trade, and in the cultural sphere. Tunisians are the group of Arab immigrants who are most assimilated in German society. The average duration of stay of Tunisians in Germany is 2–3 times longer than of the other Arabs[29]. As a rule, Tunisians more easily obtain the prolongation of their visas in the German institutions working with foreigners, due to a better knowledge of the German language. Many Tunisians seek to remain in Germany – by 2001 about 12 thousand Tunisians had received German citizenship. About 25 thousand immigrants from Tunisia lived in Germany in 2001.

Egyptians, like Tunisians, hold a privileged position in the Arab community; their number had reached 14 thousand people by 2001. They are for the most part competent workers, teachers, scientists, doctors, and engineers as well as students, whose number doubled from 2 to 4 million people within the period of 1991–2001[30]. Christian Copts represent a special group among the Egyptian immigrants; they appeared in Germany for the first time in the 1970s. Nowadays Copts are for the most part junior scientific staff and students working and studying at various universities of Germany.

Altogether Moroccans, Tunisians, and Egyptians belong to the category of immigrants who have arrived in Germany for economic reasons, namely with the purpose to find work. The group also comprises a part of the Iraqis, Algerians, and natives of the Persian Gulf countries.

The second large group of Arabs immigrated to Germany for political reasons.

One should particularly single out the Palestinians, who numbered about 100–150 thousand people in 2001, by the estimates of various experts. The current growth of the figure has resulted from the aggravation of the situation in the Middle East, although the German authorities check the immigrants from Muslim, notably Arab countries with redoubled zeal after September 11, 2001.

The first immigrants from Palestine appeared in Germany in the early 1950s; they set foot on German land not for political reasons, but with the purpose of training and engaging in commercial activity. Refugees wishing to obtain the status of the settler (asylum seeker) appeared in the Federal Republic only in 1967 and especially in the period from 1979 to 1990. The number of these Palestinian refugees was estimated at 70 thousand people, 50 thousand of them came from Lebanon and 20 thousand from the Palestinian territory occupied by Israel.

As to the immigrants from Lebanon, a rather large group of Lebanese moved to Europe, notably to England, France, Italy, and Spain during the civil wars on the territory of Lebanon in the period from 1975 to 1989. A rather small number of Lebanese got into Germany – basically through family reunification.

In the 1990s, following an aggravation of interrelations between Jews and Palestinians, a new group of refugees arrived from the territory of southern Lebanon.

At present approximately 35 thousand Palestinians live in Berlin, the others are dispersed throughout the country[31]. They maintain few contacts with the other Arabs; within the community they are divided by the religious principle, forming religious groups, such as Druze, Sunnites, Shiites, and Christians.

Although the educational level of Palestinians is rather high, they cannot receive high-school education in Germany by virtue of a number of restrictions imposed by the German authorities; therefore they mostly keep restaurants and groceries. Practically all the Arab cuisine restaurants in Germany belong to Palestinians. Such restaurants, mainly of Lebanese cuisine, are open in Berlin, Frankfurt, Düsseldorf, Stuttgart, and some other cities. They represent "eastern oases" with marble halls, fountains, carpets, and furniture made of expensive types of wood. Small snack bars trading the Arab shawarma[32] (sandwich-like wrap usually composed of shaved lamb, goat, chicken, turkey, beef, or a mixture of meats) are also very widespread. Since Palestinians and Lebanese belong to the category of political refugees, the unemployment rate among them reaches 50%[33]. This is another reason for the high degree of isolation of Palestinians, in comparison to Tunisians and Egyptians, in the German society, aggravated by the unstable position of the refugees and the watchful attitude on the part of Germans, especially after the events of September 11.

Algerians are another numerous group of immigrants to Germany. They appeared on German territory for the first time at the end of World War II. The next wave of immigrants from Algeria arrived in Germany during the struggle of this country for independence from France. However, after Algeria gained national sovereignty in 1962 many Algerians returned home. In the 1970s young Algerians arrived in Germany for the purpose of university study or in search for work. In many respects it was a secondary migration from France. Moreover, in 1974 the socialist GDR signed a special agreement with Algeria on the use of Algerian workers at German enterprises[34].

In the period between 1991 and 2001 the number of immigrants from Algeria in Germany actually doubled – from 9 000 to 17 200 people. However, these immigrants were mostly refugees who arrived in Germany because of the civil war in Algeria.

Another large group of political refugees in Germany are the Iraqis (at present their number reaches 51 thousand people), who arrived there following the war in the Persian Gulf. The majority of the Iraqis have higher education and belong by the social status to the category of the self-employed. They are mainly doctors, translators, journalists, scientists, writers, and art workers. The Iraqis have the biggest number of cultural societies in Germany. It was they who organized the Arab music festival which was held successfully in large German cities in 2001. The Iraqis have adapted rather well in German society, whereas their interrelations with the other Arab communities are basically maintained in the cultural sphere.

Yemenis and Sudanese, who appeared in Germany in the 1980s and 1990s, can also be attributed to political immigrants. However, their number is relatively insignificant – 1 586 and 4 697 people respectively.

Hereinafter the authors will examine the sex and age structure of Arab immigrants.

About 80% of all the Arabs living in Germany are people under 45 years old, the share of bachelors among them reaching 70%[35]. The absolute majority of the immigrants are males. Their share makes up 74%. Women therefore account for only 26%. The share of men is the highest among the Algerian immigrants – 81% and the natives of Egypt – 76%, while among the Moroccans the share of women makes up 39%, and Tunisians – 34%. This is explained by the fact that the inhabitants of these countries, as a rule work in Germany longer than Arabs from other countries and hold better posts. Many of them seek German citizenship. Therefore after a certain time their wives come to them, frequently with children. Nevertheless, the stay of the majority of immigrants is restricted in time, which determines the necessity to save as much money as possible while working in Germany. The upkeep of a family requires great expenses for housing, feeding, health services, etc. While living alone, denying themselves everything, the immigrants can save much greater sums. The conditions under which some immigrants live in civilized Germany are rather spartan. Although in this European country it is officially forbidden to let a one-room apartment to more than two tenants, in fact one room frequently accommodates many more people simultaneously, especially when illegal immigrants are concerned. Very frequently an apartment is rented from Arabs who, in turn, had rented it from a German, and then re-let it to Turks or other foreigners. In the case that an immigrant works at a major enterprise, he is granted a place in a hostel.

As a rule the life of Arabs in Germany reminds one of life in an Arab country. The Arab community in Germany is rather isolated by virtue of its traditions, which differ enormously from the European ones and, especially from the German traditions characterized by extreme pedantry, discipline, and order in everything. Usually the children of the Arab immigrants marry among themselves, the share of heterogeneous marriages does not exceed 10%. If an immigrant succeeds in opening his own business – a restaurant or a small store – he usually employs his relatives there. The situation of women is especially hard. On the one hand, they almost always receive a visa with a check forbidding them to work. This is the so-called "Nur zur Begleitung des Ehegattens" visa (only to accompany the spouse). On the other hand, the Arab husbands forbid their wives not only to work outside the house, but even to go shopping by themselves. Hence a narrow circle of communication of the majority of Arab women, enormous language problems, and complete isolation from German society. The language barrier is a major problem not only for women, but also for very many male immigrants. If they do find work, then it is a job that does not require knowledge of the language, except for 20–30 basic terms related to production. Knowledge of the spoken German language (not to mention the literary one) is actually entirely absent, hampering closer contacts with the local population. Moroccans represent an example of this aspect. As it has already been mentioned in this research, the majority of Moroccan immigrants in Germany are Berbers, who do not know the literary Arab language and communicate among themselves in their dialect. This brings about the isolation of the Moroccan community from the Arab cultural environment, as the language barrier limits their contacts with the Arabs from other countries as well. At the same time, Berbers in Germany speak a wild mix of German and Berber languages, unintelligible to anyone but themselves. The Berber children, born in or moved to Germany in early childhood, speak German, but do not know the

Arab language, i.e. they find themselves torn off from their historical national roots.

Another important factor hampering the assimilation of Arabs in Germany is the difference of religious beliefs. Although officially Germans treat Islam with respect and allow the construction of mosques, at the everyday level Moslems frequently arouse aversion, especially after the events of September 11, 2001, which triggered in the minds of many inhabitants of Germany an association of Moslems, especially Arabs, with terrorists.

In Germany there are three basic layers of attitude towards the immigrants.

Official authorities represent the first level. Despite the urgent need for the inflow of foreign labor, in 1981 Germany adopted a law restricting the inflow of immigrants. According to this law, each of the 16 German states had certain quotas for the admission of immigrants, reaching 13% in the better-off states (Bavaria and Baden-Württemberg), and 8% in the less affluent states (mainly, in Eastern Germany). Thus, the average quota throughout Germany added up to 10%. The duration of stay of the immigrants is also restricted. Firstly, in order to get a work permit it is necessary to obtain a relevant paper from an enterprise or company, stating that the enterprise or company in question is interested in this very employee. Secondly, according to German laws, people who have been working in Germany for 5 years acquire additional rights, such as, for example, an entitlement to provision of old-age pensions. Therefore most enterprises are interested in the fluidity of foreign labor, restricting the duration of work of the foreigners to 4 years and 11 months at most. Under these conditions it is almost impossible to find a permanent job. The wife of an immigrant can obtain the right to work after 4 years of joint stay with the spouse in Germany only if there is special request for her from the enterprise or company. Undoubtedly, we consider the cases of official work, whereas many immigrants find illegal work, mainly at building sites, but in this case they are deprived of all rights altogether, they earn much less than official workers and live in continuous fear of being exposed and expelled out of the country.

Although Germany does recognize the need to use foreign labor, it simultaneously seeks to restrict the inflow thereof. In Germany the problem of unemployment is quite acute, under these conditions Germans rather than foreigners are offered to fill the vacancies. Finally, the German authorities as well as the authorities of other European countries are aware of the danger that the virtually not increasing and growing old population of Europe might be gradually absorbed and replaced by the rapidly increasing population of Asia and Africa. Already at present almost half of pupils in the primary classes of German schools are foreigners.

Under these conditions Germany's authorities should attempt to toughen the immigration laws of their country in every possible way.

Germany's former leader, Helmut Kohl, repeatedly declared in his interviews that Germany was not a country of immigrants. His successor, Gerhard Schröder, appeared to take a more loyal stand towards the immigrants. He declared Germany needed labor migration; nevertheless it would introduce restrictions on admission of political immigrants and refugees. The basic trends of Germany's migration policies in the following years were to be:

1. An attempt to replace the immigration from the South by that from the East, i.e. from the countries of Eastern Europe. The inflow of labor from Poland, Czechia, Slovakia, former Yugoslavia, and of late repatriates from Russia and Central Asia was growing steadily within the period of 1991–2001.

2. Strengthening the control over illegal migration. This problem has become an urgent one for Germany in the last years, as refugees from zones of armed conflicts penetrate into the country through different channels, be it from Kosovo or the Middle East. The German authorities treat these people very harshly, expelling them out of the country very quickly. A German sociologist, Hermann Uihlein has made an interesting observation that only Germans give such people the formulation "illegal", "Schwarzarbeiter", automatically putting them outside the law. The French call these people "sans-papier", i.e. those who do not have the relevant documents, the English use a similar formulation: "undocumented persons". Spaniards and Italians dis-

play the softest attitude towards the "illegal" immigrants, calling them "clandestinos" or, respectively, "clandestine" – meaning "one who lives with us"[36].

Since illegal immigrants live outside the law in Germany, they increase the social instability of German society and stimulate criminality. In Stuttgart, for example, many illegal Arabs work as drug dealers.

3. <u>Fostering the integration of immigrants in the German society</u>. This means accustoming the natives from notably Muslim countries to the values of the German culture, obligatory study of the German language, encouraging the coming of the immigrants' children to Germany at an earlier age, etc. All this is done in an attempt to slow down the objective process of absorption of European culture by the Muslim one – the process which has affected Germany in the last years. All these trends of migration policies were reflected in the immigration law approved on the whole by the German parliament on March 22, 2002, and carried into effect on January 1, 2003.

Hereinafter we shall try to evaluate the changes of the immigrants' situation due to the adoption of this law.

Prior to the adoption of the law	After the adoption of the law
• The so-called immigrants (Asyl) could stay in Germany for many years. • Immigrants with temporary visa could claim the hardship allowance. • The immigrants' children could reunite with their parents in Germany without relevant education or knowledge of language up to the age of 16. • Jobs for highly qualified specialists were "held back" for Germans, despite the availability of the relevant staff in the midst of immigrants.	• The relevant authorities should consider the situation of every immigrant in an accelerated way, suppress all the abuses, and insist, wherever necessary, on their departure (this clause would largely affect the interests of political refugees from the territory of Palestine, Iraq, the Sudan, and from other conflict zones). • Entry of political immigrants should be limited. • Foreigners should be given an opportunity, subject to their qualification, to take all the jobs unclaimed by the applicants from amidst the local population.

Prior to the adoption of the law	After the adoption of the law
• The quantity of new jobs for the immigrants was limited. • The majority of immigrants did not know the German language, or knew it insufficiently. • Scientists and highly qualified specialists had as few chances to get a job as laborers. • The members of the immigrants' families faced huge difficulties during their adaptation and integration into the German society.	• Payments of hardship allowances to unemployed foreigners should be reduced. • All the immigrants coming to the country are to study the German language first of all. • The relevant authorities should draft and implement special social programs on the adaptation of immigrants in the German society. • The chances of integration of the immigrants' children in the German milieu should grow due to the restriction of age for the reunion with parents to 12 years (the children who speak German before coming to their parents, make the only exception) • The arrival of adult children and numerous relatives to the immigrants living in Germany over a long period of time shall be restricted.

Thus, the German government encourage labor migration; this referred notably to highly qualified specialists, who were granted greater opportunities under the new law.

The immigration policy of the new German chancellor Angela Merkel appears to be aimed at active development of education opportunities for immigrants. "Children and young people, irrespective of origin, should have the same opportunities in education, schooling, higher education and employment," the chancellor said. Merkel regretted that in Germany educational achievement and social origin were linked. "This link must be broken," she said. German president Horst Köhler noted that all religious communities sought to provide a good future for their children and stressed that the most important prerequisite was good education[37].

Concerning the attitude towards the immigrants on the level of public consciousness of Germans, one can state a rather high level of tolerance and desire to help the natives of other countries and culture to adapt in Germany. Ad hoc committees and associations working with immigrants, including Arabs, are established almost in every city of this country, where these people live. Numerous works are published, advocating the ideas of poly-cultural consciousness and benevolent treatment of different nationalities. This literature is distributed free of charge in libraries, at special actions organized together with the representatives of national communities, including the Arab one. There are marked days of culture of different peoples, offering the opportunity to familiarize with the way of life of this or that nation, to taste the national dishes, to listen to the national music, and to buy goods made by people from different countries. Teachers at school make no difference between the German and foreign children. Moreover, parental committees carry out an active work with the mothers of foreign children, involving them in school actions.

At the same time, cases of sharply negative attitude towards foreigners, especially towards the non-Europeans, for example, to Muslims, occur quite frequently at the everyday level. Thus, in the milieu of intellectuals this is manifested mostly in conversations, while in the lower social layers even acts of violence towards the Turks, Arabs, and Africans occur quite often.

Hereinafter we shall cite an example which befell an acquaintance of ours, M. from The Sudan. This young man, who turned 17 in 2002, came to Germany in 1996 with his parents. His father had found a job with a bakery at Pforzheim. The family lived in a small village near Pforzheim as the housing accommodation was cheaper there. The boy attended a German school; he had learnt German perfectly by 17 and studied well at a high school. However, the attitude of some villagers to The Sudanese family was sharply negative. On a village holiday two inhabitants of this locality were returning home, having taken an excessive doze of alcohol. One of them stumbled over a root and hurt his head as he fell. Together with his companion they decided that it would not be bad to use that occasion "to do a bad turn" to the damned Africans who hinder the genuine Germans to live. They picked up a metal rod, smeared it in blood, and declared to the police that the Sudanese M. had attacked them in the wood with a rod and broken the head to one of them. The boy has been brought to trial. M. denied everything, but had no alibi for that evening, according to him he simply went for a walk. The young man faced imprisonment, of which he was rescued by the daughter of the alleged victim: she admitted to having spent the evening with M. The father's reaction was so violent that the girl was forced to move temporarily to her aunt to Stuttgart. The sympathies of the local population were with the father who had forbidden to his daughter to see the "dirty Arab", although the defendant himself behaved most decently and kept silent about his meeting with the girl, even under the threat of incarceration.

The idea "Germany for the Germans" still persists amidst the representatives of different social layers, thus the formation of bicultural and multicultural consciousnesses shall take more than one decade.

Summarizing his research, the authors come to the following conclusions:

1. As to the quantitative scales of the Arab migration to Germany, one can assume that it shall increase in the next years by virtue of a number of factors, notably the ageing of the German population and a constant decline in the share of able-bodied citizens. On the other hand, the pauperization and destitution in many Arab states, aggravation of the unemployment problem largely related to the accelerated growth of population in many Arab nations as well as the aspiration to increase one's standard of living shall prompt the moving to Germany of huge masses of population from the less developed to the more developed countries, in particular, from a number of countries of Africa and the Arab East, the process forming an integral part of globalization.

2. Labor migration from the Arab and African countries to Germany, alongside with migration from other states, such as Turkey, Yugoslavia, etc., had been a necessary component of development of the German economy and has played an important role in the acceleration of the reproduction process in Germany (altogether in the period from 1954 to 2000 Germany was visited by 31 million immigrants from the various countries)[38]. For all that, the rigid immigration legis-

lation was preventing the immigrants from realizing their potential completely, affecting their social status, hindering the assimilation in the German society, and maintaining the isolation of most Arab communities.

3. The Arab immigrants in Germany have been engaged mainly in the kinds of labor unclaimed by the Germans (work in the extractive industry, at the conveyor, unskilled work, etc.), nevertheless, a certain part of the immigrants (notably from Egypt and Iraq) constituted highly qualified staff who had, for political or economic reasons, left their countries, where they might have undoubtedly brought benefits. Thus, for example, Egypt is already forced to import engineering staff. Accordingly, the consequences of migration are rather non-uniform for the Arab states. On the one hand, the financial position of a significant part of their population is improving, the foreign exchange reserves of the donor countries are growing due to remittances from abroad, and the unemployment problem is being alleviated. On the other hand, the outflow of qualified personnel from Arab nations impairs their economic growth.

4. The impact of Arab immigrants and Arab culture as part of Islamic culture upon German society tends to grow steadily. The German government and German public have realized the inevitability of this process in the last decades and seek to organize it and to avoid "dissolution" of German culture and German mentality in the Muslim values, limiting simultaneously the quantitative scales of this process. The efforts of German society during the last years of the 20th century were aimed at accelerating the assimilation of the immigrants in which Germany is interested, to the German milieu, instead of merely applying prohibitive and restrictive measures. At the same time, manifestations of an extremely negative and intolerant attitude towards immigrants, especially those from Arab and African countries, down to violence, are frequent on the plane of individual consciousness at all the social levels.

5. The second generation of immigrants, born and raised in Germany (1,5 million out of the 7,3 million of immigrants in Germany were born on the German soil), is a carrier of two languages and a

116

representative of two cultures – the Islamic and the European ones. The children of immigrants perceive most deeply the ideas of tolerance, i.e. forbearing and respectful attitude towards all the nationalities and consequently by their views and way of life they are representatives of that new poly-culture, which to a various degree is being formed throughout the world. In this respect migration exerts the strongest positive effect on the destiny of the world altogether.

[1] This part of the monograph was prepared with the financial support of the Russian Foundation for Humanities Project 09-02-00547a. / Раздел исследования подготовлен при финансовой поддержке РГНФ в рамках научно-исследовательского проекта РГНФ "Формируемые образы и реальные возможности российско-африканского «сырьевого взаимодействия» в многополярном мире". 09-02-00547a.

[2] World Development Report 2000/2001. Oxford, 2000. P. 275.

[3] Manuel de statistique de la CNUCED.2002.NU.N.Y.et Geneve, 2002. P. 25.

[4] Exportmärkte Deutschlands. Köln, 2002. S. 6.

[5] Ibid. S. 7.

[6] Oil Information 2001. OECD/IEA. Paris, 2002.

[7] Ibid.

[8] http://www.destatis.de

[9] http://www.gtai.de

[10] http://www.gtai.de

[11] БИКИ, № 97, 30.08.2003. С. 13.

[12] http://www.destatis.de

[13] http://www.gtai.de

[14] http://www.gtai.de

[15] БИКИ, 16.11.1999. С.7.

[16] http://www.gtai.de

[17] Ibidem.

[18] This part of the monograph was prepared with the financial support of the Russian Foundation for Humanities Project 07-02-02020a / Раздел исследования подготовлен при финансовой поддержке РГНФ в рамках научно-исследовательского проекта РГНФ Денежные переводы мигрантов в стратегии формирования положительного образа России: сравнительный анализ. 07-02-02020a.

[19] Трудовые ресурсы стран Востока. М., 1987, с. 323.

[20] Herbert U. Geschichte der Ausländerpolitik in Deutschland. Munchen, 2001, S. 27.

[21] Ibid. S. 31.

[22] На пороге XXI века. Доклад о мировом развитии 1999/2000. Всемирный банк. М., 2000. С. 214–215.

[23] http://www.xe.com

[24] На пороге XXI века. С. 218–219.

[25] http://www.bamf.de/cln_092/nn_442522/SharedDocs/Anlagen/DE/Migration/Publikationen/Forschung/Migrationsberichte/migrationsbericht-2007,templateId=raw,property=publicationFile.pdf/migrationsbericht-2007.pdf

[26] Santel B. Integriert oder randstandig? Zur wirtschaftlichen Situation von Einwanderen in Deutschland. In. IZA, No. 1, 2002, S. 24 (Bonn).

[27] See, for example, H. Uihlein. Menschen in der Illegalität – ein vernachlässigtes Problem. In: IZA, No. 1, 2002.

[28] Ausländer in Deutschland. Berlin, 2001, No. 3. S. 7.

[29] Regulierung und Wechsel Beziehungen zum Arbeitsmarkt, SAMPF, Arbeitspapier Nr. 6/01, Zentrum für Sozialpolitik der Universität Bremen. S. 12–13.

[30] Ausländer in Deutschland. No. 2, 2001. S. 10.

[31] Ibid., S.11.

[32] http://en.wikipedia.org/wiki/Shawarma

[33] Preis L. Internationale Migration, Bielefeld, 2001. S. 128.

[34] Neues Deutschland. 03.04.1975.

[35] Ausländer in Deutschland. No. 2, 2001. S. 14.

[36] H.Uilein «Menschen in der Illegalität – ein vernachlässigtes Problem», In: IZA, Münster, No. 1, 2002. S. 40.

[37] http://news.webindia123.com/news/ar_showdetails.asp?id=710170122&cat=&n_date=20071017

[38] B.Santel «Integriert oder ranständig?» In: IZA, N 1, 2002, Münster. S. 24.

Chapter 3. FINANCIAL FLOWS BETWEEN GERMANY AND AFRICA

3.1. New trends in German official development assistance to Africa

In 1970, the UN made a decision that the industrially developed nations were to allocate 0,7% of their gross domestic product annually as official development assistance (ODA) to the states of Asia, Africa, and Latin America. The Organization for Economic Cooperation and Development (OECD) was founded in the same year, including 21 most developed industrial countries of the world, including Germany.

One should immediately make a reservation that the total amount of the common development assistance granted by the OECD member states in general has never reached the quota of 0.7% of the GDP established by the UN.

In 1970 the share of assistance in the GDP of the OECD countries amounted to 0,35%, by 1980 it had increased to 0,37%, and declined steadily thereafter – to 0,32% in 1995 and 0,22% in 2000[1]. However, in 2007 the total ODA share of the Development Assistance Countries (DAC) reached 0,28%. In 2008, total net official development assistance (ODA) from members of the OECD's Development Assistance Committee (DAC) rose by 10.2% in real terms to USD 119.8 billion – the highest dollar figure ever recorded. It represents 0.30% of members' combined gross national income[2]. Fig. 6 shows the change of ODA share in gross national income (GNI) of DAC members since 1990.

Fig. 6. DAC members' net ODA since 1990[3]

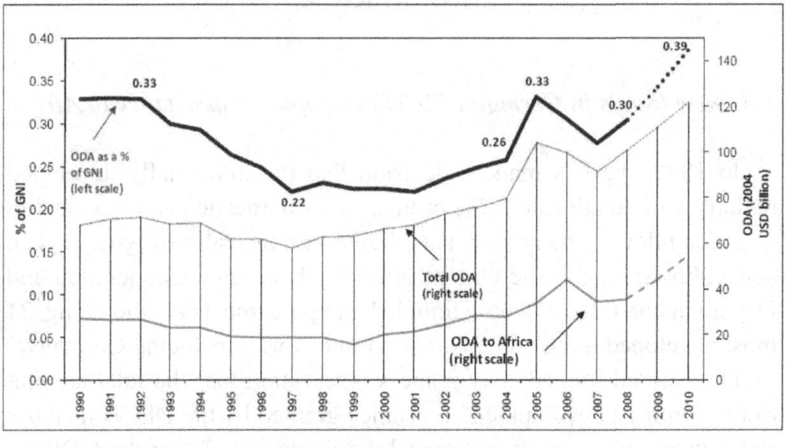

Source: OECD, 30 March 2009.

The share of ODA in Germany's GDP in 1970 was less than the aggregate of all the OECD states: it equaled 0.32% in that period; however, the relevant indicator reached 0.43% by 1980, to drop thereafter, yet to a lesser degree – to 0.33% in 1996, and to 0.26% in 1998, whereas by 2001 it even increased to 0.27% of Germany's GNI[4].

As to the total volumes of ODA granted by the world's industrial countries to developing states, and the share of this assistance in the GNI, these indicators are summarized in Fig. 7 and Fig. 8.

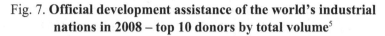

Fig. 7. **Official development assistance of the world's industrial nations in 2008 – top 10 donors by total volume**[5]

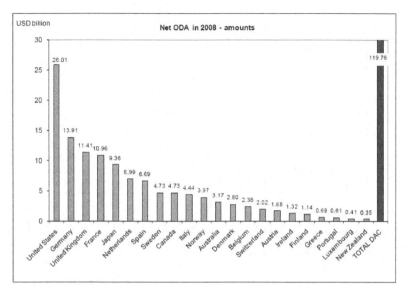

Fig. 7 shows that out of all OECD members Germany was preceded only by the USA as the ODA donor in 2008. The overall amounts of German ODA, however, were comparable with those of the United Kingdom and France, which ranked respectively the third and the forth. However, jointly Berlin and London provided less official assistance funds than Washington alone.

Germany maintained the leading position as ODA provider in the European Union in volume but not in the terms of percentage of its GDP.

Fig. 8. Official development assistance of the world's industrial nations in 2008 – top 10 donors by percentage of GNI

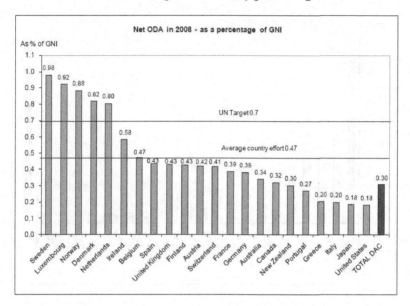

Fig. 8 demonstrates that only 5 countries: Sweden, Luxembourg, Norway, Denmark and Netherlands met the commitment stipulated by the UN in 1970 as to the share of assistance in the GNI (0.7%), and even exceeded it. The largest volume increases (Fig.7) came from the United States, Germany, the United Kingdom, France and Japan.

As regards the ODA share in the GNI, Germany holds the 14th place in the list. In terms of absolute value of the granted assistance ($13.91 billion) Germany occupies the second place among the OECD countries (after the US). Germany's share in the total ODA of the OECD member nations in 2008 amounted to 11.6%.

Official German authorities repeatedly declared that help for self-help was the Federal government's pivotal goal. It was obvious that the goal could not be accomplished unless the efforts of the under-privileged part of the urban and rural population of the recipient countries were enlisted. Furthermore, self-help required certain conditions for its realization, including the freedom of socio-political activity, self-government, and legal security as well as state institutes to serve the underprivileged.

Special attention is drawn to the need to employ comprehensively the principles of market economy, to strengthen the private sector in the process of development. Financial aid is strictly differentiated by countries and groups of countries.

The following criteria for granting aid have been established to this end:

– the countries belonging to the group of the least developed by the UN classification receive aid as donations;

– the countries most affected by the rise in prices in the world market and not included in the number of the least developed countries, receive long-term (50 years) loans at low interest (0.75% annually) with a 10 years grace period;

– the relatively developed or having significant foreign-exchange revenues developing countries receive loans at 4.5% annual interest, for the period of 20 years with a 5 years grace period;

– other developing countries receive loans with the term of 30 years, at 2% annual interest, with a grace period of 10 years.

About half of the Federal Republic's commitments of financial and technical assistance are accounted for by the poorest of the developing countries, special priority among them being accorded to the 39 least developed countries of the world.

The cited principles of granting ODA continue to apply by and large even now. The only important addition to them would be Germany's utmost support to the NEPAD initiative (New Partnership for African development) based on the neo-liberal doctrine, ideas of globalization, and recognition of the leading role of the entrepreneurial initiative.

The initiative puts in the forefront the ideas of strengthening the democracy and "good governance", combating corruption, and familiarizing the continent with the information revolution and the latest technologies. Specifically, the initiative is designed to ensure the rate of growth of the African GDP at a level of 7% by 2015 and thus to halve the number of Africans living below the poverty line, to reach the school education coverage of all the children of school age and to reduce by $^2/_3$ the infant mortality rate by 2015. Germany has actively worked within the framework of the "G8" towards the drafting a complex of efficient financial, economic, and organizational measures capable of securing the achievement of the objectives scheduled in the program. The BMZ participates directly in the drafting of German approaches to the NEPAD program; its state secretary, Uschi Eid[6], has declared that in the near future Germany would participate firsthand in securing the conditions for the implementation of this initiative.

Meanwhile, Germany, like other Western countries, is attracted by the opportunity to share the burden of African reconstruction with the Africans, under the assumption of the determination proclaimed by the African leaders to assume the responsibility for the continent's future, to expand the internal African sources of development, to implement more widely the principle of inter-commitment and mutual advantage in the relations between Africa and the West. Germany takes the same approach to the aid. The major donors, to whom Germany also belongs, are not in the least inclined to increase essentially their contributions. Germany has significantly increased its ODA share in the country's GNI lately – it rose from 0.26% in 2001[7] to 0.37% in 2007[8].

At an international conference in Monterrey (Mexico) Germany, along with other members of the European Union, pledged to increase the development assistance by $7 billion, half of the increase being earmarked for the African countries.

Generally, a redistribution of the funds appropriated within the framework of assistance for the benefit of the least developed African states was observed in the last decade of the 20th century. Meanwhile, the changing economic situation in Africa induces Germany to resort to various "unconventional" forms of financial backing, for example, to debt cancellation.

What are currently the ODA sources in Germany? 70% to 80% percent of financial resources come from the BMZ, while the rest of the funds – from the federal states and other ministries and departments (for example, humanitarian aid is allocated through the Ministry for Foreign Affairs). The means assigned by the federal states to support refugees from developing countries during the first year of their stay in Germany also refer to the development assistance. The share of ODA granted free of charge to the states of Asia, Africa, and Latin America reached 25% by the beginning of the new millennium.

Assistance provided by private German citizens and religious organizations does not belong in Germany to the ODA category.

The reduction of the ODA share in Germany's GNI in the 1990s can be linked to at least two factors:

– unification of Germany and drastic growth of expenditures on the development of the eastern states

– collapse of both the Soviet Union and the socialist camp, and granting by Germany as well as other industrial powers, so-called "official assistance" (OA) to the European states with transitional economies.

Although the policies of the developed countries theoretically did not allow for an opportunity of reducing ODA due to the growth of OA, that is what actually happened, as the European countries, notably Germany, were concerned with the political and socio-economic situation of their immediate neighbors, the countries of Eastern Europe and Russia. In the author's opinion, the proportions between Germany's ODA and OA tend to shift even more towards the latter following the accession of new members to the EU.

As to the distribution of official development assistance by such categories as bilateral and multilateral aid, approximately $^1/_3$ of Germany's ODA is granted under multilateral and $^2/_3$ – under bilateral aid programs.

As to the structure of the granted aid, in the 1990s it underwent noticeable changes, characteristic for all the OECD countries, including Germany.

Table 9
Changes in the ODA structure in the 1970s and 1990s

Sector of economy	1975–76 (%)	1996 (%)
1. Social and management infrastructure	20.2	30.2
2. Economic infrastructure	10.5	23.4
3. Agriculture	8.1	8.4
4. Industry	13.6	3.4
5. Extraction of raw materials	18.9	5.3
6. Abatement of natural disasters and other accidents	1.0	5.1

Source: www.oecd.org

As the table 9 demonstrates, in the 1990s the assistance to the development of such branches of economy as industry and extraction of raw materials dwindled sharply (by a factor of 4) – from 32.5% in 1975–76 to 8.7% in 1996. This probably resulted from the growth of the inflow of direct foreign investments of the industrial powers, which replaced for the most part the ODA. The assistance for the development of the agrarian sector of economy remained nearly unchanged, whereas the flow of ODA for the development of the social and administrative infrastructure increased by a factor of 1.5, and by 2.2 times – for the development of the economic infrastructure. A developed economic infrastructure is a necessary condition for the penetration of foreign capital into a country; it has therefore been accorded increasingly more attention under ODA programs in the last years.

As to the development of the social infrastructure, the assistance there is provided basically for the development of primary education, health services, and a family planning program. Despite an increase of this sector's share in the OPR structure, the appropriated funds are still insufficient to solve the basic social problems of the developing countries. According to German experts, the shortage of funds for primary school education reaches 75%, for the basic medical care – 65%, and for family planning programs – 20%[9].

An essential (5 times) increase of the ODA share assigned for overcoming natural disasters and other kinds of accidents is worth mentioning. In Germany's case this increase was twelve-fold – from 0.4% in 1976 to 5% in 1996[10].

The officially proclaimed priority goal of the development policies of Germany's Federal government consist also in helping the developing countries – especially in Africa – to secure their self-sufficiency in food production. Therefore the projects and programs of rural development, besides food aid under ODA, accounted for 39.4% of all the government obligations regarding the bilateral financial and technical assistance in the 1990s, while for the countries south of Sahara this figure reached 57.7[11]. These programs envisage projects to increase the agricultural and handicraft production, developing adapted technology to this end, creating and strengthening the relevant national consulting services, research and financial institutions, developing cooperative supplying-marketing associations and trading networks in rural areas, creating there the necessary infrastructure, etc. Implementing such programs presupposes a high level of management qualification, special significance in this respect is therefore attached to advance training of national experts in the field of management.

The projects in the sphere of education rank next by significance in the Federal Republic's assistance (approximately 25% of the total amount of bilateral government obligations). In this area priority is accorded to professional training programs (more than 60% of the overall BMZ expenditure on education) and to projects in the field of higher education (nearly 190 in number) in such specialties as engineering, natural sciences, and agriculture.

Special projects on protection of environment and resources have acquired increasing significance in the framework of bilateral cooperation. The Federal government therefore supports programs aimed at improving the systems of land-utilization, afforestation, and combating desertification and erosion.

Other trends of state cooperation include power engineering projects (reduction of the use of wood for fuel, decrease of the import of energy carriers, wide use of internal inexhaustible energy sources) and family planning (mainly carrying out wide explanatory and consulting work). Significant attention is also paid to the projects aimed at stimulating women's implication in the development.

The main ODA funding source (up to 70%) is the budget of the Federal Ministry of Economic Cooperation (BMZ). Other funds come from the budgets of other ministries, separate states of the Federal Republic, the EU budget as well as from the German Development Bank (KfW).

Hereinafter the authors of the monograph will address the problem of geographic distribution of aid, notably of the share received by the African states.

In the second half of the 1990s Africa ranked second by volumes and share of the ODA received from Germany, after the Asian region. The years 1996 and 1997 made an exception, when African states received more ODA from Germany than the Asian ones, the increase being predominantly on account of the North African region. Overall, the share of Africa in the German ODA varied during the period at issue between 31% and 37%, i.e. one–third of the total Federal Republic's bilateral official development assistance was granted to the African states. The countries of Africa south of Sahara received from ⅔ to ¾ of the German ODA. As to the total amounts of aid, this indicator (in terms of constant prices of 1998) reached its peak – $1 594 million – in 1996 (including $1 098 million to sub-Saharan and $496 million to North Africa), then it began to decline and dropped to $1 239 million in 1999 (983 million and 255 million respectively), approximately 1.3 times less than the maximum amount of Germany's aid to Africa. However, one should make a reservation that the reduction of the German ODA to Africa was largely determined by the overall reduction of the volumes of German development assistance from $4 523 million in 1995 to $3 738 million in 1999, or by a factor of 1.2. Structurally, however, in the second half of the 1990s the share of Africa dropped by 3%, while the shares of Asia, Europe, and America increased, though relatively little.

As regards the new decade, the data comes in terms of constant prices of 2000, permitting to point out some features characteristic of

128

the new century. Thus, the overall German ODA in terms of current prices stood at $5 030 million in 2000, while in 2001 it registered $4 990 million (the similar indicators in euro registered €5 458 million in 2000 and €5 571 million in 2001). Remarkably, in 2008 the overall ODA granted by Germany made up nearly twice as much as in 2001 – $13 910 million[12]. The ODA share in Germany's GNI did not exceed 0.27% in 2000 and in 2001, while the share of aid granted on bilateral basis increased from 53% in 2000 to 57% in 2001.

Meanwhile, the Federal Republic's OA granted to the countries with transitional economy increased from $647 million in 2000 to $687 million in 2001, or by 6.1%[13].

As to the distribution of German ODA in sub-Saharan Africa in 2005, the picture evolved as described hereinafter:

Fig. 9. **Distribution of German ODA in sub-Saharan Africa in 2005**[14]

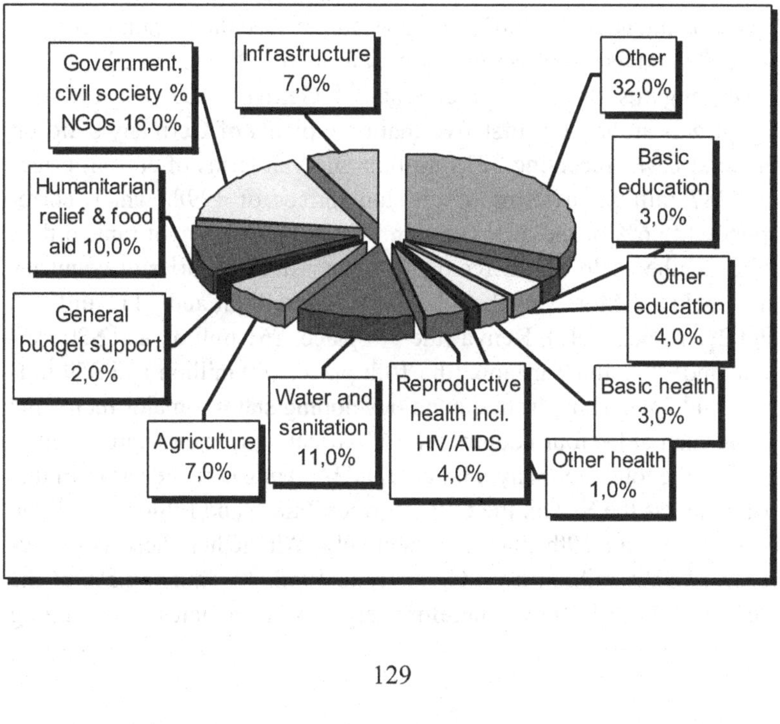

In 2005, the most recent year for which data are available by sector, Germany increased its shares of ODA to sub-Saharan Africa going to basic education, basic and reproductive health, infrastructure, and government and civil society. It was the only G8 country that contributed its equitable share of funding on water and sanitation. The one-third share of German aid to the region reported as 'other' includes €93 million (US$115 million) in multi-sectoral aid, €46 million (US$57 million) for micro credit and financial systems and €20 million (US$25 million) on industrial development.

In 2006, sub-Saharan Africa received 33% of German assistance, which is higher than at any time in the past decade and which represents a marked increase in Africa's share compared with 2005.

The budget of the Federal Ministry for Economic Cooperation and Development (BMZ), which accounted for 60% of German ODA in 2006, was €4.18 billion (US$5.2 billion) in 2006, an increase of 8.2% over 2005. A further increase of 7.6% to €4.5 billion (US$5.6 billion) was foreseen for 2007. In 2007, BMZ stated that for sub-Saharan Africa 'It is intended for 2007 and 2008, to increase the commitments for financial and technical cooperation by around 25% each year'.

As regards the major recipients of German ODA, in 1988–89 Egypt was among the first five main recipients of Germany's aid on bilateral basis, receiving $218 million ODA in terms of current prices or $287 million in terms of constant prices of 1998, which corresponded to 6% of the total German bilateral ODA. Egypt ranked then third on the scale of aid recipients. The list of 10 priority countries also included Morocco (the 8th place, $84 million and $111 million, and 2% respectively), Kenya (the 9th place, $61 million and $80 million, and 2%), and Tanzania (the 10th place, $60 million and $79 million, and 2%). Thus, from the ten developing states – major recipients of German aid – four countries were African, and their share stood at 12% of the total Germany's bilateral ODA. Tunisia ranked 15th in this list, whereas the Sudan, the DRC (former Zaire), and Ethiopia took the 17th, 18th, and 19th places respectively. Altogether these countries received $198 million from Germany in 1988–89, equaling 5% of the German bilateral ODA. Therefore, eight African states were among

130

the 20 major recipients of Germany's aid on bilateral basis in 1988/89, receiving altogether 17% of the German aid, or $758 million in terms of constant prices of 1998.

In 1993–94 the situation somewhat changed. Egypt continued to head the list of African aid-recipient countries, but went one step down – to the 4th place. Simultaneously the volume of German ODA rendered to this North African country increased and amounted to $308 million. Zambia ranked eighth ($125 million and $124 million respectively), while Mozambique ranked tenth ($119 million and $118 million). Ethiopia went down from the 19th place in 1988/89 to the 11th ($109 million and $107 million); Tunisia and the DRC left the list of 20 priority recipients of German aid altogether, whereas Tanzania, Morocco, and Kenya moved to the 17th, 19th and 20th places respectively. Thus, in 1993–94 the 20 major recipient countries of the German ODA already numbered 7 African states – Egypt, Zambia, Mozambique, Ethiopia, Tanzania, Morocco, and Kenya. The share of these states in the total ODA had reached 15%, amounting to $853 million, i.e. by 12% more than at the end of the 1980s.

In 1998–99 the first twenty recipients of the German aid included only 5 African states: Egypt ranked fifth; the total amount of Germany's ODA to this country dropped to $132 million, i.e. more than by a half as against 1993–94. Tanzania went up to the 6th place in the list; the amount of aid to this country increased to $88 million. Morocco ($73 million) and Mozambique ($68 million) ranked 11th and 12th respectively. However, while the amount of aid rendered to Morocco increased by $10 million or by a factor of 1.2, the German ODA to Mozambique shrank almost by a half in absolute value terms. Zambia found itself on the 18th place with $57 million, i.e. 2.2 times less than in 1993–94. Altogether 5 African countries – Egypt, Tanzania, Morocco, Mozambique, and Zambia – received $426 million from Germany by way of ODA in 1998–99, or 11% of Germany's total bilateral ODA.

It is noteworthy that in 2006 the major share of the means appropriated by Germany for Official Development Assistance was received by Nigeria. Table 10 shows ten major recipients of Germany's ODA in 2006[15].

Table 10

Top 10 Total ODA Recipients 2006
(commitments in $mln)

1	Nigeria	1.710,81
2	Iraq	388,17
3	Zambia	287,54
4	China	244,85
5	Cameroon	228,11
6	Serbia	202,49
7	Egypt	140,61
8	Afghanistan	117,99
9	Morocco	104,49
10	Viet Nam	86,75

Thus, 5 African countries are present in the list of the 10 major recipients of Germany's ODA in 2006 – Nigeria, Zambia, Cameroon, Egypt and Morocco. Together they received an amount of $2 471 million; more than half of the sum fell on Nigeria ($1 710 million).

Germany's development assistance increased by just 2% over the period 2004–2006; this is largely the legacy of the previous administration. Germany needs to increase its assistance to Africa by $869 million each year from 2007 to 2010 in order to get on track and reach the 2010 target of $5 754 million (constant 2004 prices)[16].

In the summary another important point concerning the aid is to be mentioned. Although the budget of the BMZ tended to reduce in the period between 1993 and 2000, the volume of financial resources coming to Germany by way of interest on the credits granted under the ODA, was on the contrary growing. Thus, in 1993 these receipts constituted DM 1.44 billion, while in 1997 they already reached DM 2.19 billion[17].

Thus, a special report prepared by the BMZ experts maintains that "Germany reaps no economic benefits whatsoever by abandoning the granting of aid, on the contrary, it brings about appreciable losses"[18].

The report states that although ODA's main goal is combating poverty, destitution, famine, illiteracy, and illnesses, the donor countries, including Germany, also derive economic benefits from it. The ODA is being spent, for example, on remunerating German experts in the developing countries, including the African ones, besides the goods from the donor-country are accorded priority in the local national markets. The ODA plays a part of a "door opener" for the export of German production and promotion of German capital in the African markets.

According to the BMZ experts, abandoning the ODA could lead to the loss of 240 000 jobs for the inhabitants of Germany, while the export from this largest country could dwindle by €5.5 billion – an amount exceeding the entire volume of ODA in 2001. The experts maintain that "the economic benefit from the ODA for the German economy is much higher than one could assume"[19].

Thus, the official development assistance granted by the OECD member nations to the African states can by no means be referred to pure charity. The industrial powers, including Germany, create the necessary conditions for promoting their goods, capitals, and services in the African markets by managing distribution, structure, and volumes of aid. Providing assistance permits the developed states to impose certain political demands, conditioning the granting of aid on the "agreeable" or "disagreeable" nature of the political regime in this or that country. In other words, granting ODA in the epoch of globalization in many respects serves as the precondition for promoting transnational corporations and banks in the new markets of the developing states and involving the latter in the modern system of international labor division, advancing thereby the interests of a limited circle of world economy subjects.

3.2. Direct investments

The inflow of foreign entrepreneurial investments to Africa grew steadily till the mid-1970s. The former colonial companies ceded to more powerful monopolistic associations – Transnational corporations

(TNC). In the second half of the 1970s, however, the new inflow of foreign direct investments (FDI) slowed down, while in a number of countries (Nigeria, Libya, etc.) it even gave place to the repatriation of capital because of a surge of nationalization of foreign property. That was one of the reasons of the gradual reduction of Africa's share in the total amount of direct investments by TNC in the developing world – from 27% in 1975 to 14% in 1985.

In the early 1980s the African governments started to adjust their development patterns under the influence of the economic crisis. The concepts of liberalizing the economy, utmost development of the market mechanisms of management, implementing the macroeconomic stabilization as an antirecessionary basis of structural reforms prevailed. The official circles of the countries of Africa abandoned the former unilaterally negative treatment and the underestimation of the constructive functions of the foreign private capital, triggering the alleviation of the investment regime. The policy of bans, restrictions, rigid regulation of the TNC activity, which prevailed in the 1960s – 1970s, ceded to a state policy aimed at their attraction, working out compromises while cooperating with foreign investors.

The foreign direct investments entailing such highly rating assets as capital, technology, management experience, and means of production in one "package", are welcomed and actively attracted by all the African countries. Nonetheless many of them, notably the least developed countries of Tropical Africa (despite the undertaken attempts to improve their investment climate) continue to be relatively unfavorable in the world FDI market, owing to a number of fundamental reasons. Besides the instability of political regimes, the basic factors in this connection are the low level of domestic savings, limited nature of local markets and of the solvent demand, low GDP growth rates, backwardness and in most cases unsatisfactory functioning of the physical, institutional, and financial infrastructure, chronic balance of payment deficit, debt crisis and the acutest deficiency of foreign currency related to it, limiting the transfer of profits and the repatriation of capital, absence or acute shortage of qualified personnel, high production costs, universal corruption, bureaucratic abuse of discretion, and in some cases the lack of appreciable progress in implementing market reforms.

After the monetary crisis of 1997–1998, many economists recommended to the countries of Asia and Latin America to focus on attracting direct investments from abroad, aimed at increasing the stability of their economic development. However, the experts of the Institute for World Economies at Kiel consider that the interrelation between the inflow of foreign capital and the rates of increase of the GDP has not been researched sufficiently hitherto.

In their opinion, globalization by means of stimulation of the migration of the investment capital has acquired a special significance since the early 1990s. Since approximately the same time there has been observed a growth in the share of the developing states in the total volume of the received foreign direct investments (FDI). The role of FDI for a number of such countries has been discovered to be more significant than for the developed states. The experts from the Kiel Institute reject the widespread opinion that the concentration of FDI occurs in several relatively large developing countries which had registered certain progress. Among the successful recipients there are also a number of relatively small states with a low level of per capita income. An inference is drawn that "in essence all the developing countries have a chance to become attractive" to the foreign capital.

However, the local politicians have yet to determine the most productive methods fostering the amplification of the FDI inflow. Many traditional measures, among them the liberalization of the investment legislation and assistance to business development, can hardly become a panacea. Such reforms as privatization of public enterprises seem to be a more efficient means of attaining the proposed objective, but even they are to be completed with innovations in the neighboring areas (for example, initiatives in the sphere of competitiveness) so that the receipt of FDI could bring real benefit to the national economy.

According to German scientists, the significance of the factors traditionally considered to be contributing to the FDI is not to be accepted without any reserve. Thus, the market capacity which used to be considered as the major element in making a decision to direct large investment resources to it, hereafter can appear less significant. The politicians obviously exaggerate the role of regional integration as a powerful and long term stimulus for FDI.

Scientists from the Kiel Institute consider that the measures on promoting investments will prove to be inefficient unless the bases of economy in the recipient country encourage the inflow of foreign capital. Tax and financial stimulus for foreign investors can bring more harm than benefit if they trigger a competition between the countries – potential recipients of FDI. This could force them to agree to the introduction of a plenty of privileges and indulgences for the investors, resulting in the end in significant financial losses and a distorted allocation of capital by countries and regions. Economists are increasingly inclined to support the conclusion that the competition to attract investments, based on the use of special stimulus, is inefficient. However, in practice this opinion of the experts is hardly ever taken into account.

Under the conditions of globalization there is seemingly a transition from the FDI seeking for the most attractive market to a new type of FDI, the major factor for which is the competitive ability of the local producers. In these circumstances governments of the developing countries are compelled to create such immanent values which provide real advantages in the struggle for the FDI. These include, for example, additional investments in education and other spheres of human development, establishment of a base permitting to master developed foreign technologies in a rapid and trouble-free manner, and rendering modern kinds of services to the growing business. The correct choice of the trade policy plays a pivotal role. Liberalization of trade in production means and intermediate production shall foster the success in attracting FDI, which shall come there, where they can be used with the greatest efficiency.

The German scientists warn against expecting too much from the inflow of foreign capital to a country. A FDI boom is observed in the world, but investments on the whole continue to remain a predominantly national phenomenon.

136

In many respects the FDI surpass other forms of capital inflow. An important characteristic of FDI is the risk sharing, which is of great importance in financing the developing countries. This aspect has acquired special significance after the monetary crisis in Asia and some other regions. It has demonstrated once again that the FDI are a more stable form of financing than other kinds of capital inflow. However, the FDI's positive influence on the economic growth of a country is not to be considered as something self-evident. The relation between the FDI and the total investments as well as the economic growth in the host country is not a direct one and is subject to further studying.

Having characterized the role of foreign investments in the economy of African countries, the authors will dwell in more detail on the quantitative characteristics of the German FDI in Africa:

– The total volume of the foreign direct investments in the economy of the countries of Africa (the SAR excluded) invested predominantly by TNC reached $75.3 billion by 1998. It amounted to only 1.8% of the global volume of FDI and to 6.1% of their total amount throughout the developing world. The FDI inflow equaled $9.7 billion in 1999 (as against $7.9 billion in 1998) – the lowest indicator among all the regions of the world;

– The aggregate amount of Germany's FDI in Africa totaled $4.7 billion by 2000. The biggest investments were made by German companies in the economies of the following countries: SAR – $2.5 billion, Libya – $0.8 billion, Nigeria – $0.3 billion, Egypt – $0.25 billion, and Tunisia – $0.2 billion. Altogether in 1998 the volume of direct German investments in the countries of Africa amounted to $0.5 billion, whereas in 1999 it dropped to $0.35 billion as a result of the world financial crisis; however, it increased again to $0.51 billion by 2001. The share of German FDI directed to Africa constitutes less than 1% (more precisely, 0.76%) of Germany's total direct investments. The countries of the European Union account for more than 66% of Germany's total foreign direct investments, 24.2% fall to the share of the US, 4.3% – to Asian countries[20].

As to the branch structure of the German direct investments, the most attractive economy sectors of the foreign countries to German investors were the sphere of services, including trade, (49.3%) and industry (48.4%).

Despite the relatively small amounts of inflow of the German FDI to Africa, it would be wrong to consider it as a region of poor investment opportunities. The African countries differ essentially by the size of the domestic market and economic growth rates, by the availability of natural resources, by the development of entrepreneurship, and by the level of political stability. These distinctions predetermine the investment opportunities of the region's states.

A sizeable domestic market, gradually developing infrastructure, cheap labor, low raw material prices, political regimes securing the unobstructed transfer of profits abroad, tax privileges on the part of the local government, reduced tariffs for electric power and other services of the public sector, an opportunity to use the local financial resources, and availability of electronic means of communications can be attributed to the main factors determining the geography of placement of the German private capital in the countries of Africa.

The complex of mineral raw materials in Africa attracts the largest volumes of German FDI. The present stage of development of Africa's raw material economy is distinguished by the fact that in spite of economic and political risks, the long-term investments of TNC in the production of some types of mineral raw materials and energy carriers, notably the World Ocean bed production continue to grow. Thus, the investments of German companies in the production of investment goods in the majority of the African states are insignificant, whereas more than 60% of investments are accounted for by the extractive industry.

Private money-market loans received against state security are quite frequently used for the financing of the newly created oil-and-gas and mining complexes. Simultaneously, the non-joint-stock participation of the TNC is increased in the field of exploration and development of new deposits, in the sphere of final processing, transportation, and sales of the production. Their return to the African raw material sector occurs through granting loans, through concluding management, license, and consulting contracts, through active help in marketing, by means of contracts for leasing the previously national-ized enterprises and otherwise.

The high capital intensity of the projects and the degree of risk in the countries with an unstable investment climate force the TNC to combine their forces and resources within super-consortia, to venture on partnership with national state agencies. Moreover, the reliability of FDI in the production of strategic raw materials and energy carriers is generally secured by a wide participation in the investments of the public or half-public companies of the capital exporting countries.

At the same time, Germany, being dependent on energy supplies, is trying to expand independently its investments in this branch over-seas, notably in Africa.

An example hereto is the growth in the volume of Germany's direct investments in oil and gas production in Libya, Algeria, and Egypt. In 2001, Germany's investments in this branch of the abovementioned countries totaled $200 million. Whereas Germany's relations with Egypt and Libya have a relatively long history, as far as the "sharing of the Algerian pie" is concerned, Germany was somewhat late – it was outstripped by such countries, as France, Italy, and the US.

Nonetheless, due to a deterioration of links between Algeria and its traditional partner, France, following the nationalization of the oil-and-gas branch in 1971, the Algerian government already then ap-pealed to Germany for the implementation of ambitious industrial pro-jects estimated at $30 billion. Algeria embarked on the epoch of con-struction of "turn-key" objects in its relations with Germany. Now the Germans are watching closely the situation in Algeria, which gradu-ally makes the enterprises of its state sector more open for foreigners and undertakes the establishment of joint ventures.

The Association of Algerian and German businessmen was set up in 1997, proceeding, in particular, to defreeze the unimplemented con-tracts of the eighties for the sale of gas to Germany. According to the Algerian newspaper El Watan[21], the mistakes committed by the Alge-rian leadership and its sluggishness resulted in the loss by Algeria of a market of gas in Germany and in the deterioration of the bilateral rela-tions.

The evidence of transition from the wait-and-see to a more active strategy of the German corporations in the area of FDI in minerals production has shaped since the end of the 1980s, as the demand for them was generated by fundamental improvement in the sphere of science and technology and the prices for them, as per estimates, are to grow in the long term: gold, platinum, diamonds, rare metals (Zimbabwe, Guinea, Botswana, Gabon, the Ivory Coast, Ghana, Namibia, the DRC, Niger, and Burkina Faso). In the mean time, the growth of German investments in the traditional copper-nickel, iron ore, and aluminum industries has not been observed yet.

At the same time, a rather high share of investments in the manufacturing industry is another peculiarity of the German FDI in the countries of Africa. FDI can also play an important role in the development of the export-oriented branches of the manufacturing industry of the African countries, as the experience of some of them convincingly testifies. Notably Morocco and Egypt attract significant investments in electronics, car assembly, textile and woodworking industries, and in production of building materials, using their achievements in reforming the economy and such specific advantages as availability of the relatively prepared and cheap labor and geographical proximity to Europe. For example, the German BMW concern declared the opening of its first car assembly factory in Egypt in 1997.

The FDI share is particularly high in the manufacturing industry in the SAR, which is Germany's main economic partner in Africa.

It has already been mentioned above that the total amount of Germany's FDI in the SAR had reached $2.5 billion by 2000. However, the German literature justly pays attention to the inaccuracy of the statistical data on direct private investments in the SAR. According to some experts, Germany's private investments in the SAR reach in fact $4 to $5 billion.

Approximately half of the German investments are made in the branches producing investment goods – mechanical engineering, electrical engineering, exact mechanics and optics, whereas a quarter – in the main branches of heavy industry and in the production of semi-finished goods (chemistry, metallurgy, etc.). At the same time, investments in the branches of the extractive industry and production of commodities are hardly of essential significance here. Altogether more than 70% of the total German direct investments in Africa in such branches as electrical engineering, chemistry, automobile manufacturing, and mechanical engineering are accounted for by the SAR. In other states of the African continent, on the contrary, investments of the German companies in production of investment goods are insignificant; more than 60% of investments are represented by the extracting industry[22].

One of the important directions of activity of the German private capital in Africa is its increasingly wide participation in the establishment of joint enterprises. This is determined by the fact that a joint enterprise provides a foreign investor with a stable position in a country's domestic market in the long-term plane, leads to a certain reduction of the production costs owing to the privileges on the part of the national government, raises the company's reputation in country, etc. The German companies therefore perceive an important means to strengthen their positions in Africa in the establishment of joint enterprises. More than 500 German companies function at present in the South African region alone, employing 80 000 people at their enterprises. Joint ventures are set up by such largest German companies as BMW AG and Daimler AG, Hoechst AG (chemistry and pharmaceutics), Lufthansa AG, the Siemens company, and many others[23].

Hereinafter the authors will cite some examples of German-African joint enterprises.

Within the struggle against HIV/AIDS, a joint South African-German enterprise for the production of condoms is to be built in the SAR, the city of East London, East Cape Province. It is going to become the largest one in Africa with initial annual output amounting to 100 million pieces.

A joint venture Condomi Africa Ltd is formed with the participation of a well-known German company from Cologne, Condomi AG. "Ferrostaal Investment" from the German side and a consortium of black businessmen, "Kula Industrial Investments", as well as the

"Women's Development Bank Investment Holdings" from the South African side are also going to participate in the joint venture.

According to estimates, the annual demand for condoms on the continent adds up to 3–4 billion pieces. The new factory in East London can increase its facilities significantly in time, depending on the demand; it is able to perform orders from many African countries.

The plans of the joint venture cover not only industrial activity, but also carrying out workshops on issues of family planning and struggle against HIV/AIDS in the SAR[24].

A large delegation of German businessmen came to Algeria in June 1999. The Algerian government was inclined to restore the economic ties, even more so as the Germans brought a specific project with the value of almost half a billion in US dollars.

In November 1999, it was proposed to create a joint venture between the Algerian oil-and-gas state company Sonatrach[25] and Germany's BASF. The tasks of the joint venture with investments in the amount of $200 million covered, in particular, the production of propylene in Tarragona, Spain. Sonatrach, owning 49 percents of the capital, is to provide the transportation of 420 tons of Algerian propane thereto annually, by its own ships, for 12 years.

An arrangement was achieved in November 1999, that all the Algerian-German economic projects are to be coordinated by a special office resuming its activity.

Furthermore, the German party unblocked the credit of DM36 million (€18,4 million) allotted for cooperation in the field of environmental protection, job creation, and conducting joint scientific researches. Twelve more joint projects were on the agenda, including the building of a factory for the production of household chemicals under the license of the German Henkel company. An investment of $60 million was envisaged for that enterprise.

According to El Watan, Germany intends to master together with the Republic of Algeria the markets of Maghreb and of the Middle East. Negotiations with Algerian businessmen are underway for the formation of approximately 30 objects in this region by means of joint ventures[26].

It is also worth mentioning that such largest German banks as Deutsche Bank, Commerzbank and Dresdner Bank cooperate with the business banks of the SAR dealing in servicing the current commercial operations of the joint German-African companies.

In its turn, Germany's federal government supports the activity of the German private capital in the SAR by creating manifold and well organized tools, securing tax privileges and indemnification to private investors in case of nationalization of their property or emergence of any other claims. State insurance of foreign investments of the German companies, conclusion of intergovernmental agreements on protection of private investments, and tax privileges, among other things, function as components of this system.

A special place in the system of investments protection in Africa and, in particular, in the SAR, is held by the state insurance company Hermes providing payment of indemnifications to private investors of capital from the federal budget in case of nationalization, changes in the country's policies, wars, introductions of restrictions on the transfer of profits, etc. Simultaneously the Hermes experts conduct marketing researches and determine the attractiveness of a certain country in terms of activity of the German private capital.

German experts elaborated a special five-degree scale according to which they determine the attractiveness of a country to the German capital. The application of this scale will be hereinafter exemplified to the SAR.

Table 11

Degree of attractiveness of the SAR as a German trade and economic partnership

Name \ Rating	1	2	3	4	5
Labor potential	O				
Standard of well-being				O	
Economic growth		O			

Name \ Rating	1	2	3	4	5
Economic stability				O	
State of the trade balance		O			
Direct investments from Germany			O		
Costs per unit of output		O			
Export risk				O	
Degree of corruption spread			O		
Credit rating				O	

Source: Deutschlands Exportmärkte. P. 214.

The scale has 5 degrees, 1 corresponding to the estimation "excellent", 2 – to "good", 3 – "satisfactory", 4 – "below the average", and 5 – to a "bad mark".

As the table proves, the SAR has a high rating in such indicators as labor potential, economic growth, state of the trade balance, and costs per unit of output, a satisfactory evaluation on the level of direct German investments and degrees of the spread of corruption, and quite low ranking by the standard of well-being of the population, economic stability, export risk, and credit rating. This is largely related to the complexities of the country's socio-political situation, which can aggravate at any moment, notwithstanding the slight recent stabilization. Furthermore, the ways of further transformation of the SAR into a part of the global economy, including the mechanisms of redistribution of income as well as the economic and social consequences of the undertaken reforms, leave the issue of the SAR achieving the status of an equal right partner open[27]. However, despite the difficulties in the economical and socio-political development of the South African Republic in the last decade, this very country will most likely maintain its leading positions in commercial and economic relations with Germany in the forthcoming 10 years.

In the last years the insurance system has been completed with a number of the new provisions encouraging the German businessmen's activity in Africa. Thus, the part subject to insurance against risks of the exported capital has been increased by 5% and makes 95% of its total amount now. The state insurance has also been extended over a part of the reinvested profit from the insured capital which had been invested overseas. Now the German investors are entitled to apply for the extension of insurance over the capital formed due to the reinvestment of profit and amounting to 50% of the initially insured direct investments[28].

State warranties of private investments are supplemented by a system of agreements on investment protection concluded by Germany's government with the countries of Africa on a bilateral basis. These agreements are aimed at securing the inviolability of the German private investments in Africa against the possible nationalization, internal economic reforms, or changes in the legislation. A new agreement of this kind was signed between Germany and the SAR in 1997[29].

Such form of state stimulation of the German private investments as tax privileges granted by special tax laws also underwent essential modification. In the SAR in particular, these privileges include tax relief, creating a 50% reserve not taxable for 6 years out of the proceeds, preferential crediting of joint enterprises with a share of national capital of more than 50%, granting interest-free loans for developing the branches of vital significance to the economy of the SAR, and establishing free economic zones. Simultaneously Germany concluded an agreement with the SAR, which prevents double taxation of the German businessmen's income[30].

The majority of countries of North Africa adopted investment legislations meeting the interests of both national economies and the Western investors. The most liberal investment legislation was adopted in Egypt and Tunisia. Thus, in Egypt the foreign capital is completely secured against nationalization. Foreign capital enjoys special privileges in 16 branches of economy, such as cultivating the land, poultry farming, cattle breeding, industry, constructions, tourism, processing and storage of agricultural commodities, marine and air transport, housing construction, real estate operations, oil refining and transportation, construction of hospitals and medical centers, water-pump stations, venture capital, development of computer technologies, social sphere, and securities market. In this manner all the companies operating in these spheres (the foreign ones included) are exempted from the profit tax during five years. The foreign capital invested in new industrial areas and new urban centers, is exempted from the profit tax for 10 years. Should foreign companies choose areas outside the Nile valley as their sphere of action, then the grace period is extended to 20 years. The companies whose activity is not related to priority branches of economy can also obtain similar privileges. All the new companies, including the foreign ones, with the number of workers more than 50 people, benefit from a 5-year-exemption from all taxes.

In Tunisia tax privileges lasting up to 10 years are accorded to export companies. The import of materials and equipment is exempted from taxes. Investments on preferential terms can be made in the tourism sphere, including construction of hotels, health protection, education, environmental protection, waste processing, science, and new technologies. Thus, the inflow of foreign capital is welcomed in most spheres of national economy, as it is laid down in the investment legislation of Tunisia[31].

The Federal Ministry of Economic Cooperation (BMZ) elaborated a special program promoting the investment by small and medium-sized German enterprises in the countries of Africa, including the SAR, through granting long-term credits on favorable terms. These credits can be used both for the implementation of specific projects and for marketing research. The maximum amount of the credits makes €1.5 million. They are granted at the annual interest of 2.5% for the poorest countries (for the SAR, being a country with a relatively developed economy – at 3.5%) for a term of up to 15 years with a maximum grace period of 5 years[32].

Tourism deserves special attention on the part of foreign investors.

The African continent offers a rich palette of tourist sights, some of them (beaches, ecotourism) similar to the ones offered by other countries, while certain kinds of tourism exist only in Africa (safari-tourism). The majority of African countries can satisfy only a part of the tourism demand for goods and services (accommodation, foodstuffs, and leasing of automobiles) by means of local companies, while the remaining backlog demand awaits the inflow of foreign investments.

Tourism has since the last decade become one of the major directions of Germany's cooperation with the SAR. The SAR, a country with unique natural conditions, attracts tourists from all over the world, including Germany. Development of cooperation in this sphere is crucial for the dynamic development of the South African economy altogether. The fact is that direct investments in the industrial sector do not lead to a rapid job expansion in the SAR. On the other hand, the tourist sector deals with this task quite successfully, as investments in this sector recover fast, creating the preconditions for the development of mixed branches – social and industrial infrastructure, transport, construction, and local industry. The development of tourism also promotes the creation of jobs for the South Africans at the place of their residence – in immediate proximity to the tourist objects, reducing thereby the intensity of internal migrations of the population down the lines village-town, town-city-capital and alleviating the unemployment problem.

In 2002-2003 the contributions of German businessmen to the development of tourism in the South African region exceeded €1 billion[33].

Training African experts in the field of commerce is another mainstream of German activity. The German experts developed a special Human Development Program in 2000. Its essence is reduced to training the staff of African businessmen, which undergo special preparation in African countries, and thereafter in Germany, at companies having close business ties with Africa. The basic form of training is business–workshops. In the period 2000–2001 alone, 400 South African businessmen received vocational training[34].

Thus, in the last years Germany has been actively cooperating with the African states in the most different directions, including the establishment of joint ventures, development of infrastructure, tourism, staff training, etc. As to the geographic distribution of Germany's FDI in Africa, they are to preserve the selective, differential approach and the tendency towards the development of economic ties with a limited number of countries (the SAR, Libya, Egypt, Algeria and Tunisia are among Germany's main partners at present) in the next decade.

Summarizing this section of the paper the authors arrive at the conclusion that the influence of foreign capital, including the German one, upon the formation of the cost and natural-material structure of the GDP of African countries is determined by its place in the economy and its role in the internal capital formation. On the whole, the external investments represent a substantial contribution to the accumulation fund of a number of developing states of the region, especially of economically least developed ones, which is confirmed by the statistics of their national accounts.

The inflow of foreign capital, both state and private, in monetary and commodity forms, smoothes down the disproportions in the cost and natural-material structure of the public product. The larger the part of investments directed to the productive capital, notably the fixed capital, ensuring the progressive structural transformation of the public reproduction, the more significant is the role of the foreign capital. Investments in the fixed and the circulating capital secure the real accumulation due to the importation of the machinery, equipment, chemicals, construction materials, etc., which are not produced in the country importing the capital, due to the import of technology, "know-how", and services of qualified experts.

This can be illustrated by Zimbabwe, Egypt, Morocco, Nigeria, Botswana, Swaziland, Mauritius, and other countries. Direct investments of TNC in these countries provide unique opportunities to form the structure of the fixed capital. The combination of the capital itself, advanced technology, and management experience within the investments can be manifested in the acceleration of the capital-accumulation rate, re-equipment, in raising the technological level, and the efficiency of the means of labor. The importance of such investments goes therefore far beyond their nominal volume.

The connection of the local manufacturers to the technically developed dynamical TNC sector promotes the deployment of the adjoining branches and market links, the inter-branch capital turnover, alleviating the lack of capital at the macroeconomic level. Capital export draws apart the accumulation limits in the country of its application as the additional demand for labor emerges, the training and retraining of the local staff is stimulated.

Involving additional local material and labor resources in the economic circulation, TNC and other foreign companies foster the absolute increment of the economic potential of the recipient countries. It is especially important that foreign investments, unlike the national ones, are usually completely provided with currency, technical and material elements, etc., permitting to increase appreciably their efficiency, labor productivity, and the quality and range of the output produce, to stimulate the modern trends in developing the industry, and sometimes the conception of essentially new advanced technology production kinds (computers, communication facilities, electronic components, etc.).

One should not forget, however, that along with the complication and increase in the science-intensity of production, the increase of the related level of vertical integration within the TNCs, their contacts with the local manufacturers tend to subside. The decline of the ties is conditioned both by the inability of the local producers to supply the foreign companies with the required production components and by the counteraction of these companies to the advanced technology "drain". Consequently, the stimulating effect of foreign investments on the technological level and on the scales of capital accumulation in the importing country is reduced; there emerges a threat of transition of some branches of national production under the "foreign" control, of escalation of competition between the local enterprises[35].

The effect of foreign investments is also leveled by direct withdrawals from the national entrepreneurial income, since a significant part of it is repatriated from the recipient countries. The reverse capital outflow by way of profits, interests, and dividends is not always overlapped by its counter inflow, as the resident foreign companies ac-

149

tively use for capital financing both their own savings and the local borrowed funds.

3.3. Policies of German Banks in Africa

The African region became in the 1990s a sphere of regular credit, loan, and investment activity of the leading banks of the industrially developed countries as well as of the bank groups and consortium associations thereof. The inflow of the international banking capital in the continent's countries broadens the opportunities to accelerate the region's economic development and widens the access of some African countries to contracting loans from the Eurocurrency market.

The investment expansion of transnational banks (TNBs), their groups and associations into the developing countries generated as a matter of fact a new channel of links between the young states and the world powers in the 1990s, having modified their former monetary, financial, and credit relations. A relatively efficient mechanism of influence of the industrial countries and their banks on the economy and the external economic exchange of the recipient countries started to function on the basis of the TNB credit activity. The real share of the various forms of capital export is changing. In particular, the credit channel has turned into a means of influence of the foreign banking capital on the branch structure of the recipient countries' economy and on their credit and banking sector, in the overwhelming majority of cases in full accordance with the interests of TNC and of the foreign private capital.

State loanable funds[36] play the leading role in the inflow of foreign capital to Africa. Interstate bilateral and multilateral loans come by the channels of international crediting and development assistance programs implemented by the Western states within the OECD, and by the OPEC countries since the 1970s. Development assistance is the main source of currency funds ensuring the implementation of expanded reproduction in the economically least developed countries (Chad, Burkina Faso, Uganda, Mali, the Sudan, etc.). The share of external resources in the annual investments of these countries amounts to 60–80%. Foreign assistance programs and obtaining public credits are an important channel to mobilize the resources to balance the system of external payments in other African countries as well (Morocco, Egypt, Kenya, the Ivory Coast, Zambia, etc.).

In 2000 the total amount of Germany's ODA to the developing countries totaled $4 852 million equaling 0.26% of Germany's GDP in the same year. In 2004 it made up $7 534 mln already; by the end of 2007 the figures had skyrocketed to $12 267 mln (see Table 12).

Table 12

General ODA figures of Germany[37]

	Total ODA	
	Million USD	**% of GNI**
2004	7.534,21	0,28
2005	10.082,16	0,36
2006	10.434,81	0,36
2007	12.267,13	0,37

In 2000 Germany ranked second after France by the volumes of official development assistance to the countries of sub-Saharan Africa ($1 800 million)[38]. Since then the situation had changed; in 2004 Germany held the 4th place in the list of major ODA donors with $2 235 million (after the US – $ 4 695 mln, the UK – $2 596 mln and France – $2 481 mln). In Fig. 10 the key ODA donors are ranked according to the scale of their aid increase, required to meet the respective 2010 goals marked grey[39].

Fig. 10

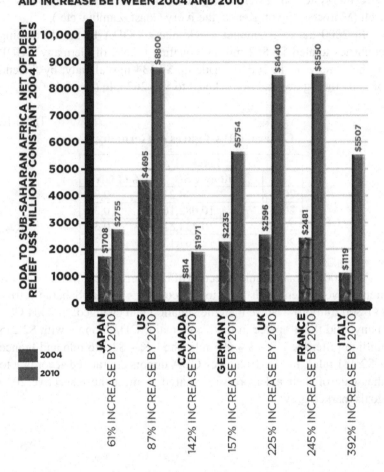

DONORS RANKED BY THE SCALE OF THEIR
AID INCREASE BETWEEN 2004 AND 2010

Official German authorities repeatedly declared that "help for self-help" was the Federal government's pivotal goal[40]. It is emphasized that the goals can not be accomplished unless the efforts of the under-privileged part of the urban and rural population of the recipient countries are enlisted. Furthermore, self-help requires certain conditions for

152

its realization, including the freedom of socio-political activity, self-government, and legal security as well as state institutes to serve the underprivileged.

Special attention is drawn to the need of comprehensive employment of principles of market economy, to strengthen the private sector in the process of development. Financial aid is strictly differentiated by countries and groups of countries.

The following criteria for granting aid were established to this end:

– the countries belonging to the group of the least developed by the UN classification receive aid as donations;

– the countries most affected by the rise in prices in the world market and not included in the number of the least developed countries, receive long-term (50 years) loans at low interest (0.75% annually) with a 10 years grace period;

– the relatively developed or having significant foreign-exchange revenues developing countries receive loans at 4.5% annual interest, for the period of 20 years with a 5 years grace period;

– other developing countries receive loans with the term of 30 years, at 2% annual interest, with a grace period of 10 years.

About half of the Federal Republic's commitments of financial and technical assistance are accounted for by the poorest of the developing countries, special priority among them being accorded to the 39 least developed countries of the world.

In 2001, Africa received about 40% of the Company's financial resources appropriated for the developing countries. The main recipients were Kenya, Somalia, the DRC, Egypt, and Mali. In the branch plane the largest part of the funds was directed to agriculture, health protection, and infrastructure (more than 70%)[41].

Private loanable capital, notably banking capital, came to Africa on a large scale in the 1970s – early 1980s. The international banks' investments in this region registered an increase of almost 30 times between 1972 and 1980. Expensive bank loans and private export credits become one of the essential components of the deepening state indebtedness and the escalation of a debt crisis in the African countries. The reaction of the creditors to the weakening solvency of the developing states manifested itself in toughening the conditions of credit and financial operations and in curtailing the relations with unreliable partners in view of a sharp increase of the credit risks. The consequence, despite the persisting great demand for borrowed funds, was a 6-fold reduction in the annual volume of crediting of the African countries in the markets of the private capital, whose core was the Euromarket (or the Eurocurrency market), namely from $2.4 billion to $0.4 billion between 1983 and 1996.

The multinational banks (TNBs) controlling the Eurocurrency market displayed a high degree of selectivity while implementing the credit policies in the African region, limiting their clientele mainly to the countries whose solvency raised no doubts.

Among the major factors promoting the penetration of the German banking capital into the countries of Africa are:

• formation of a surplus of investment capital at many German banks pushed them to expand purposefully the spheres of regular foreign investment operations, to venture upon an objectively risky and "unusual" for the majority of them extension of the sphere of their credit-loan activities as well as their networks of offices and branches over a weak, in currency and financial terms, periphery part of the world economy, namely the countries of Africa;

• internationalization of industrial production, capital, and foreign trade in the epoch of globalization undoubtedly requires an adequate system of modern international bank settlements. The territorial distribution of branches and offices of the German banks in Africa started to coincide more or less clearly with the formed trajectory of commodities and services flows generated by the activity of German companies;

• the emergence in the 1990s of a tendency to restrict the growth of regular income (and the level of the net profit, accordingly), which could be derived by German business banks in their internal credit market from traditional banking operations and transactions. Hence an urge to enter the less stable, but up-and-coming African markets;

• impossibility to conclude global international agreements on the regulation of operational activity of the banking consortia in the

Third World (particularly in Africa) because of the active opposition from the most powerful American banks. The combination of these factors forced almost all the non-American TNBs, including the German ones, to develop purposefully and to diversify their own network of foreign offices and branches, mostly outside the currently existing zones of unconditional influence of the US TNBs and of their financial and industrial groups, including on the African continent;

- the increase of the role of the own long-term interests of the German banks, in particular in relation to the diversification of the cumulative assets portfolio, to the growth of the total amount of mobilized monetary resources, to the increase in the mass and norm of profits, etc.

Meanwhile, a growing selectivity of the expansion of German banks in Africa (subject to both internal economic facts and political situation in a specific country of the region) became increasingly obvious in the 1990s as never before. Naturally, the concentration of the predominant part of offices and branches of German banks persists by virtue of these reasons predominantly in the economically most developed countries of the African continent. Objectively this very group of countries has preserved the necessary preconditions for the banks to perform stable and regular operations, to mobilize the necessary volume of internal money resources, and to obtain a cumulative mass and rate of profit in the recipient country, acceptable to a foreign bank.

For all that, the state of economy and the situation in the currency and credit-banking spheres of the recipient country are not always the main factors determining the long-term policies of German banks in Africa. A new phenomenon of the 1990s was the tendency that the countries of an "average" level of economic development and the economically least developed African countries also became objects of allocation of investment capitals of the German banks.

Being the least developed link in the economic structure of the Third World", Africa will most probably remain of little attraction as a sphere of application of the productive (industrial) TNC capital. It would seem that by virtue of these and a number of other reasons Africa cannot be an attractive region for regular investments by TNBs (especially by ones with large-scale capital) in the long-term aspect, where their new offices and branches would open periodically, the scales of the current activity would increase, the operations would diversify, and most of all the subscribed capital of their branches and affiliated companies operating there would be constantly replenished. Meanwhile, the relative reduction in the share of direct industrial investments (in the fixed capital and in the production capacities of enterprises), especially of the direct industrial TNC investments, in the total volume of the foreign capital received by Africa in the 1990s, obviously contrasted with the steady enlargement of the scales of TNB expansion, the growth of capital, and the diversification of the network of their offices, branches, and affiliated establishments in the region.

The goals and priorities of own investment strategy of transnational banks in the countries of the continent are brought to the forefront nowadays. TNBs continued the purposeful enlargement of the scales of their investment and lending activity in the region over the 1990s, although extremely unevenly by recipient countries. In the author's opinion, such tendency will objectively persist henceforth.

The investment strategy of the German banks, which are new donors and investors of the banking capital in Africa, is quite indicative in this respect.

Africa's share at the beginning of the 1980s amounted to 3.3%–4% of the total volume of all the German direct foreign investments, according to a number of expert estimates, while in the 1990s this indicator dropped to 0.5–1%. Nevertheless, the relatively steady expansion of the German banks into new, "unconventional" for them recipient countries of the region (the Arab Republic of Egypt, Chad, the Sudan, Tunisia, Morocco, Kenya, Zambia, the Congo (Kinshasa), Uganda, and Zimbabwe) persisted in this particular period. These countries became the main recipients of the German banking capital in Africa in the 1990s.

The fact that the German TNCs (engineering companies of a broad structure by their status) keep increasing their individual share holding in the large investment and industrial (mainly international) projects in the African countries, also acquires considerable significance.

156

Agriculture, ferrous metallurgy, flour-grinding, food-processing industry, and diamonds processing are among the spheres of regular activity of the German TNC in the region. The Federal Republic's government constantly grants special financial aid to the Arab Republic of Egypt, Nigeria, Algeria, Mali, Equatorial Guinea, the Sudan, Tanzania, Tunisia, Ghana, Zambia, Zimbabwe, Senegal, Chad, Cameroon, the Congo (Kinshasa), Morocco, Swaziland, Burkina Faso, Madagascar, and Libya under separate investment projects credited by the German TNBs. Thus, the powerful German Development Bank (KfW) actually joined the project financing of a number of investment projects in the region, including within the Franc Zone (for example, in Senegal) and the subsequent control over them already in the late 1980s.

The German transnational corporations had previously invested significant monetary resources in the mineral resources industry for the development of oil fields and of iron ore, bauxites, manganese, and uranium deposits. Later on the manufacturing industry also turned into a priority sphere of investment by the Federal Republic's companies in Africa.

Under these conditions the TNBs of the Federal Republic (as well as their TNCs) should have objectively attempted to oust the TNBs of other countries, primarily the French and English banks maintaining the historically formed advantages in the recipient countries, and to limit the spheres of their influence in the region, with a view to strengthen their own positions. On the contrary, they ventured to establish currency and credit links and industrial cooperation with the TNBs of France and Great Britain (as well as with their TNCs) in the 1990s; it was especially clearly displayed in the second half of the 1990s in relation to the French TNBs and TNCs. The fact is that Germany's TNBs aspire to use efficiently the experience and the filial network of the French and British TNBs, particularly to lean in case of need on the highly ramified and functionally diversified network of the French TNBs. At the same time, the formation of stable unions and associations of various types of German companies and TNBs with the companies and banks of Italy, which were represented in the credit and banking sector of a number of the region's countries in the

157

late 1990s, is worth mentioning. Italian companies and banks agree to such cooperation because of a shortage of their own considerable monetary resources; they seek to secure the possibility to perform operations in the countries of the region new to them on the basis of German banks, participants of consortium unions and associations, and correspondents thereof, in the absence of a network of their own offices and affiliated enterprises in these countries.

Unlike most of the world TNBs, the German banks in Africa venture to extend their share holding in the local development banks, specialized investment banks of long-term crediting, and development corporations. Since the second half of the 1980s they have been gaining foot in the sphere of intermediate and long-term crediting and investment banking operations in the region. In particular, since the late 1980s the Federal Republic's TNBs (primarily through mediation as well as through direct share holding of the state organizations Deutsche Entwicklungsgesellschaft and KfW) have put their investment capitals in the share capital of the major development banks in Lesotho, Mali, Morocco, Swaziland, and Somalia.

Germany's banking capital in the region had already been represented previously in 13 investment banks of development and financial (investment) companies in the Ivory Coast, Gabon, Guinea, Mali, Niger, Senegal, the Congo (Kinshasa), Burundi, Rwanda, The Sudan, Morocco, and Tunisia. Since the late 1980s Germany's banking capital has also participated appreciably in the subscribed capital of 11 private business banks in a number of the region's countries. Specifically, four such mixed capital banks operated in the 1990s in the Ivory Coast; three banks functioned in Cameroon, two – in Senegal, and two banks – in Chad.

The Arab Republic of Egypt, Chad, the Sudan, Tunisia, Morocco, Kenya, Zambia, and the Congo (Kinshasa) have figured among the countries – objects of regular application of Germany's banking capital, primarily of the private one, since the early 1990s.

Sudan and the Franc Zone countries have grown into priority zones of expansion of Germany's banking capital in Africa since the second half of the 1990s. A steady tendency towards the extension of the share holding in the investment banks of development and long-term crediting, in financial companies in Africa as well as to the establishment of in-house banks by one hundred percent of the capital, subsidiary banks, bank offices, and specialized branches (including the ones operating in the sphere of long-term investment crediting) remains characteristic of the activity of TNBs and of Germany's banking capital in the region.

A global tendency towards the internationalization of the banking was traced in Africa in the 1990s with a certain specific character.

A gradual, stage-by-stage coverage and subsequent involvement of an increasing number of the economically least developed countries into the TNB sphere of influence and control continued. Along with it, an essential diversification of the spheres of application of foreign banking investments was perceived, particularly the international banking capital's penetration into the subscribed capital of specialized investment banks of development as well as of the private investment financial companies in the region proceeded.

An interlacing of capitals of the various countries (of both state and private sectors) in the bank stock of the local business banks as well as of investment banks of development has appreciably accelerated and complicated in Africa altogether.

One of the traits of expansion of the foreign banking capital to Africa consists in the fact that nowadays banks and bank groups of a number of industrially developed countries simultaneously penetrate, and then jointly extend their presence and scales of operational activity in the mixed capital banks in the recipient country. Consequently, whereas down to the mid-1980s the African continent had been actually divided into zones of priority influence of the banking capital of certain foreign investor countries (notably France and Great Britain), nowadays international banks and bank groups have embarked on the path of long-term partnership in the credit-banking structures of the recipient countries. A steady tendency towards globalization and subsequent internationalization of the international banking capital in the region's recipient countries determined the formation of a multistage, multinational, and ultimately transnational structure of the banking business in a number of African countries. Such a structural transformation of the subscribed capital of money corporation meets the objectives and principles of collective multilateral control and influence over the economic strategy of the region's recipient countries (notably on the part of the EU).

The expansion in the volume of business of some multinational bank groups and associations of the highest transnational type (level) largely brought about a diversification of the institutional structure and an increase in the scale of operational activity of transnational banking business in the region in the 1990s.

Offices of these transnational bank groups in the African recipient countries are foreign banks (banking establishments) by their status, however in legal terms they do not belong to the banking capital of a certain industrially developed country; they represent a special segment of the international private market of capitals. In most cases such foreign banks are multinational offices of TNBs and groups thereof with mixed capital. They are jointly controlled by banking groups of Great Britain, France, Germany, and the US.

The expansion of scales of regular operations performed by the multinational (transnational) bank group SFOM[42], especially in Chad and Cameroon, has been (among other manifestations of the tendency towards the internationalization of banking in Africa) under attention since the second half of the 1980s. SFOM incorporates (consolidates) capital on account of direct share holding of the French BNP Paribas[43] (legally heading this group), Dresdner Bank AG (Germany), and of the ING[44] (Belgium).

The activity of such a global transnational banking association as the Meridian International Bank (MIB), which consolidates the capitals of shareholders from the leading countries of the Western Europe and the Arab international capital, extended in Africa in the 1990s. The headquarters of this bank are registered in Nassau (Bahamas), containing the two leading branches in New York and London. This TNB either has its affiliated enterprises or possesses the controlling stock of the local banking establishments in Burundi, Liberia, Zambia, Cameroon, and Nigeria. The Pan-African headquarters of the bank operate in Lusaka (Zambia).

This specialized bank encourages private foreign businessmen and investors from the developed countries (and their private investments accordingly) to come to the region in the most efficient ways and to deploy in the economy sectors most profitable to the investors in the recipient countries. Furthermore, the Bank supports and stimulates the development of the intra-African currency, credit, payment, financial, and banking cooperation in the various forms and spheres. This trend in the bank's activity has acquired considerable importance, since until now any two adjoining African countries having a common border, have always carried out their mutual monetary settlements and payments, in particular in the foreign trade, exclusively through the business correspondent banks of the developed states, notably of Western Europe.

The MIB managed to connect some recipient countries to the international Eurodollar market of private capitals through its diversified branch network. Simultaneously, it essentially facilitates the settlement, payment, and currency transactions of its foreign correspondent banks in those African recipient countries where its offices, branches, and affiliated enterprises operate. The branches and affiliated enterprises of industrial companies and TNCs as well as of the trading-marketing companies, which have been operating in Africa for over 30 years, have now turned into the leading shareholders and clients of the MIB as well as of its local branches in Africa's recipient countries. The bank is expanding its current credit-loan activity in Africa. It also specializes in investment crediting of objects in the field of agriculture, agrarian-industrial association, civil aviation, industrial engineering, and housing construction. The priority spheres of MIB's regular crediting in the 1990s included primarily wholesale and export trade in metals and metal ores, production of mineral raw materials, output and production of energy resources, transport sphere, wholesale and retail trade in manufactured goods and consumer goods.

The bank has accumulated specific experience in the current servicing and crediting of corporate clients in recipient countries, including the crediting of the local industrial production, new industrial investments, and of the intra-African trade, which is extremely important for most of such countries. At present the bank proposes (as one of priority goals of its current credit-loan and investment activity) its transformation into a link between the various sub-regions of Africa, in order to perform their mutual external settlements and payments, notably with a view to intensify the intra-African trade (subject to the availability of the necessary preconditions) and the intra-African monetary and financial cooperation.

Multinational bank groups consolidate their grip in the continent's countries new to them, in the various branches and spheres of their economy, on the basis of opening offices and branches, either their own, or completely under their control. Thus, in the 1990s they frequently increased to some extent the scales of crediting and investment in the local industrial production (though previously primarily in the manufacturing industry) as well as in the projects in the field of infrastructure industry, including the finance and banking infrastructure. The implementation of projects in the field of infrastructure and in the banking sector is aimed at facilitating henceforth the development of the continent's natural resources, mainly in the agro-industrial countries. For example, the construction of modern transport highways on the basis of TNB bank credits facilitates essentially the access to strategic raw material in Africa.

Such bank groups collaborate closely with the leading foreign industrial, trade, and marketing corporations operating steadily in Africa, by way of constantly granting them long-term credits, including currency loans. Thereby the necessary preconditions for the consolidation of the positions of the TNCs in the recipient countries' economies are created.

Multinational character is inherent in the banking capital. Banks of different countries come together in joint-stock banking companies and groups in Africa, getting along with each other quite well. Manifestations of increasingly close monetary and financial links between the private foreign banks of the various countries by way of subscription to the capital of the operating mixed banks, establishment by them on-the-spot of new consortium type banks with mixed capital as well as of groups, associations, and banking consortia thereof were typical in the region's countries in the 1990s.

The internationalization of the local industrial production and trade-marketing activity in the region, including the foreign trade, directly accompanied the amplification of the transnationalization process of the banking capital in the recipient countries in the 1990s. The formation of primarily mixed banking establishments, with a significant number of external shareholders and foreign investors became typical of most of them.

Banks of France, Great Britain, Germany, Italy, The Netherlands, the US, Belgium, and Luxembourg, as well as powerful multinational bank associations and groups participate on a share basis in the subscribed capital of such mixed banks.

In some cases the transnational organization of banks gets even more complicated. Thus, the French Crédit Lionnais, the German Deutsche Bank AG, the Italian Banca Commerciale Italiana, and the international (multinational) bank association Morgan Guaranty International Finance Corporation (the American TNB Bank Morgan) participate with their capitals jointly on a share basis in a number of mixed banks of the African countries. These number Société Camerounaise de Banque Cameroon (SCB)[45], Banque commerciale du Congo (B.C.D.C)[46], and L'Union gabonaise de banque[47].

The same foreign banks (excluding the Morgan Guaranty or other subsidiaries and regional branches of the Morgan Group) are the leading foreign shareholders (investors) in the Banque Tchadienne de Crédit et de Dépôts (BTCD), L'Union Gabonaise de Banque, and L'Union Togolaise de Banque (UTB).

Another multinational bank association of a similar type includes the French trade (business) bank Société générale, a Swiss TNB, the business bank Crédit Suisse, an Italian business bank, Banca Nazionale del Lavoro, and the German versatile universal Bayerische Vereinsbank. These TNBs jointly participate with their capitals in bank institutions (of various types) in Cameroon, the Ivory Coast, Senegal, Tunisia, Mauritania, and other countries, including in the local specialized national banks of development and long-term crediting.

In both the region overall and separate recipient countries the watersheds between separate foreign bank groups are inevitably displayed less clearly, while the borders and spheres of their priority influence and control are becoming obliterated and blurred as a consequence. At the same time, ever more new African countries are being involved in the spheres of influence and control of the leading TNB groups, the control of foreign bank groups over the credit-bank and money-markets of the recipient countries is getting stronger, and the mobilization of the local money and currency savings, including those of the national industrial sector, is being intensified.

TNBs and their groups use ever more flexible and diversified methods of adaptation and gaining foothold in the monetary and credit markets of the countries of Africa, implement new methods of control over the economic territories, with a view to redistribute the zones of influence in the region. The spheres and zones of influence of the transnational banking capital in Africa are extending.

The transnational banking capital, being involved in the credit-loan and investment operations in the recipient countries, is modifying its policies in the region depending on its own long-term objectives and priorities. The new nature of the long-term TNB strategy in Africa was displayed in the 1990s through involving the economically least developed countries in the sphere of their operational activity and constant influence, creating and subsequently increasing the subscribed capital of the mixed capital banks of development, of the banks of long-term investment crediting as well as of investment financial companies, transnational by their capital and activity status. Frequently these unite (consolidate) the capitals, including the public ones, of Germany, Great Britain, The Netherlands, and Italy). In a number of cases these mixed capital investment institutions are joined by such international agencies as the International Finance Corporation (IFC) and the Finance Management Overseas (FMO, the Netherlands).

In other words, the main strategic goal of the long-term policies of TNBs (including the Eurobanks specializing in Eurocurrency crediting) is being implemented in the recipient countries, by way of encouraging from without (including the mechanisms of Eurocurrency crediting) and stimulating from within the partnership of private African national businessmen, of the African state, and of the public companies of the recipient countries with the foreign banks and private foreign industrial and trading capital.

Such strategy objectively prompts the formation in the recipient African countries of a peripheral type of economy, avowedly dependent on the industrial countries. Consequently, the direct credit, monetary, and debt dependence of the recipient countries, including the enterprises and companies of the public sector, as well as of the key industries and spheres of economy on TNBs, on the international banking capital, and on TNCs will inevitably deepen. A monetary and financial mechanism of long-term partnership of a dependent, obviously subordinated type is developing and steadily recurring in practice.

The global tendency towards the internationalization of the international banking was traced with a certain specificity in Africa in the 1990s.

Unlike the majority of the world TNBs, the German banks in Africa venture to extend their share holding in the local development banks, specialized investment banks of long-term crediting, and development corporations. Since the second half of the 1980s they have been gaining footing in the sphere of intermediate and long-term crediting and investment banking operations in the region. In particular, since the late 1980s the Federal Republic's TNBs (primarily through mediation as well as through direct share holding of the state corporations Deutsche Entwicklungsgesellschaft and KfW) have been putting their investment capitals in the share capital of the major development banks in Lesotho, Mali, Morocco, Swaziland, and Somalia.

From its part, Germany's federal government supports the activity of the German private capital in the SAR by creating manifold and well organized tools, securing tax privileges and indemnification to private investors in case of nationalization of their property or emergence of any other claims. State insurance of foreign investments of the German companies, conclusion of intergovernmental agreements

165

on protection of private investments, and tax privileges, among other things, function as components of this system.

A special place in the system of investments protection in Africa and, in particular, in the SAR, is held by the state insurance company Hermes providing payment of indemnifications to private investors of capital from the federal budget in case of nationalization, changes in the country's policies, wars, introductions of restrictions on the transfer of profits, etc. Simultaneously the Hermes experts conduct marketing researches and determine the "attractiveness" of a certain country in terms of activity of the German private capital.

---

[1] www.oecd.o11rg/document/21

[2] http://www.oecd.org/department/0,2688,en_2649_33721_1_1_1_1_1,00.html

[3] http://www.oecd.org

[4] Ibidem.

[5] http://www.oecd.org/dataoecd/47/52/42458612.pdf

[6] http://de.wikipedia.org/wiki/Uschi_Eid

[7] Olsen R. German Official Aid to Africa: is there a link? Bonn, 2002. S. 102.

[8] http://www.oecd.org

[9] www.bmz.org

[10] www.oecd.org/document/61

[11] Ibidem.

[12] www.oecd.org

[13] Estimated on the basis of: www.oecd.org/danaoecd/42/1/1860346.gif

[14] http://www.thedatareport.org/pdf/germany2007.pdf

[15] http://www.euroresources.org

[16] http://www.thedatareport.org/pdf/devAssistance2007.pdf

[17] www.bmz.org

[18] www.bmz.org/report124

[19] Ibidem.

[20] Exportmärkte Deutschlands. S. 355–357.

[21] http://www.elwatan.com/

[22] www.germanchamber.co.za

[23] www.business-africa.com

[24] www.germanchamber.co.za

[25] http://en.wikipedia.org/wiki/Sonatrach

[26] Эль-Ватан. Алжир.210402

[27] *Притворов А.В.* Южная Африка и другие страны южноафриканского региона в эпоху перемен. М., 2002. С. 102.

[28] www.saen.net

[29] www.safri.com

[30] Exportmärkte Deutschlands. S. 216.

[31] Exportmärkte Deutschlands. S. 60, 232.

[32] Ibid. S. 34.

[33] www.safri.com/tourism_english.html

[34] www.safri.com/hrd_english.html

[35] *Рощин Г.Е.* Иностранный капитал в экономике стран Африки. Страны Африки 2002, М. 2002. С. 78.

[36] http://en.wikipedia.org/wiki/Loanable_funds

[37] http://www.euroresources.org

[38] www.unctad.com/report2002

[39] http://www.thedatareport.org/pdf/devAssistance2007.pdf

[40] Berliner Zeitung. 20.03.2001.

[41] Ibidem.

[42] SFOM (Société Française pour les pays d'Outre-Mer) – a Swiss holding company for the Group's associated banks in Africa (Burkina Faso, Côte d'Ivoire, Gabon, Guinea, Madagascar, and Senegal).

[43] http://en.wikipedia.org/wiki/BNP_Paribas

[44] http://www.ing.be/private/index.jsp?&lang=fr

[45] http://ebank.creditlyonnais.cm/fr/

[46] http://fr.wikipedia.org/wiki/Banque_Commerciale_du_Congo

[47] http://fr.wikipedia.org/wiki/Union_Gabonaise_de_Banque

CONCLUSION

The complex and ambiguous processes in the German-African economic relations of the 1990s were a consequence of structural changes which had affected both Germany and Africa.

The end of the 1990s and the beginning of 2000 became for Germany a period of implementation of structural reorganization of its economy following its reunification, the amplification of integration processes in the EU and its eastward expansion, and the strengthening of economic ties with the industrially developed partners, which could ensure a trade exchange at a new technological level. These factors combined have brought about a slackening of cooperation with the backward regions of the world. In particular, insufficient attention to the encouragement of activity of the German private business in Africa has become one of the immediate consequences of German reforms.

The economic crisis in many developing countries of Africa has fostered in its turn the incorporation in the 1990s of preconditions to implement a large-scale program of structural reorganization, which shall sustain its significance at the beginning of the 21st century. Thereupon the factor of economic stability in terms of developing the relations of free market entrepreneurship in the region will be a necessary condition for the expansion of Germany's economic activity in Africa, notably in the field of resuscitation of trade and investment activity of the German companies.

Germany, as one of leading members of the European Union, forms the principles of its policies towards the Third World countries, including the African ones, within the framework of the Pan-European approach. Former Germany's chancellor, Gerhard Schröder, repeatedly emphasized that Germany in its foreign policy was guided by the principle of pursuing the common interests of the EU member nations. The foreign policy record of chancellor Merkel shows her preference to convince and to discuss. A notable characteristic of Merkel's foreign policy style is her preference for teamwork, transparency, dialogue, and discretion – a style of rationality, matter of factness and low-key public appearances. Chancellor Merkel has developed a distinct mix of traditional attitudes and new approaches to German foreign policy.

The European Union, and Germany along with it, considers the "African" economic policy as a component of the EU's cooperation with the African, Caribbean, and Pacific states (ACP). While drafting the main principles of these policies, the EU takes into consideration primarily its own economic and political interests. Germany, a European country with the most powerful economic potential, has played an active part in the drafting of the main principles of these policies, fixed in the Yaoundé and Lomé conventions, and nowadays – in the renewed conventions under the Cotonou agreement.

Since the second half of the 1990s Germany (within the EU) and the developing Africa have sought new forms of cooperation. A number of negotiations took place at various levels in 1997–2007, culminated in signing a new document – the Cotonou Agreement. Germany strives to establish a partnership of a new type with the African states, with a view to create additional opportunities for German investments. From their part, the African countries expect to set up with Germany's help an efficient system promoting their economic and social development, the reduction of their external debt by its rescheduling and cancellation, and surmounting other difficulties.

Germany considers the following to be the crucial aspects in its policies of cooperation with the African states: providing assistance on preferential terms so as to mobilize the intrinsic opportunities of the countries of the African continent; comprehensive use of the principles of market economy; support on the part of the private German and local capital, especially from the small and medium-sized businesses; state support of the activity of private investors in Africa; observance by the partners in economic cooperation of the acknowledged international legal norms, including those in the sphere of human rights.

The stated principles of foreign policy of the 1990s by and large continue to apply to date. The only essential addition to them is Germany's all-out support for the NEPAD initiative (New Partnership for African Development) based on the neo-liberal doctrine, ideas of globalization, and recognition of the leading part of the entrepreneurial initiative.

Overall, despite a rather modest role of Africa in Germany's foreign trade turnover (less than 4%), one should not underestimate its significance for the economy of the largest European country. Not only does the African continent provide a considerable share of Germany's demands for raw material, but it also represents a perspective market for the leading, largely export-orientated branches of German industry. Furthermore, following the discovery of new, on the assumption of some experts, huge oil and gas fields along the African fault, Africa can become an important sphere of application of the German capital in the next decades.

For Germany, Africa is primarily a supplier of raw materials and a market for the German industrial output. An extremely low provision of the demands by its own oil and gas production rendered Germany completely dependent on the import of these types of raw material. Despite a number of actions aimed at saving fuel and energy and turning from oil to the use of other energy carriers, the growth of dependence of German economy on the import of oil and gas supplies tends to continue in the near future.

Besides the African oil, which covered more than one third of Germany's demand in certain years, the countries of Africa provide a significant share in supplies of cobalt (the main suppliers – the DRC (former Zaire) and Zambia, bauxites (Guinea), copper (Zambia, the

170

DRC), phosphates (Morocco, Senegal, and Togo), etc. The SAR plays a pivotal role as a supplier of raw materials of strategic importance for Germany, importing uranium, vanadium, manganese ore, rough diamonds, chrome, platinum, nickel, etc.

Foodstuffs, mainly cocoa-beans, tea, sugar, and coffee, continue to hold a major place in the German import from the African continent. The specifics of the German import of foodstuffs from Africa lies in the fact that an overwhelming part of the goods passes through intermediary companies, which play a pivotal role in the market; possessing a rich commercial experience and a developed system of links with both manufacturers and consumer companies, knowing well the market since as far back as the pre-war times, and having comprehensive information on it.

An analysis of the commodity composition of the German import from Africa demonstrates that new opportunities for its expansion have appeared under modern conditions, not only in the oil-refining and food-processing industries but also in the production of agricultural raw materials, and to an even greater degree regarding finished products and semi-finished goods. Germany's purchases of finished products and semi-finished goods in Africa have increased in value more than by a factor of 15 over the last thirty years. The circle of African countries supplying the products of manufacturing industry to the German market is not great so far; it is limited to the most developed by the African scales states of North Africa and the SAR.

Unlike the German import, the commodity composition of the export remained stable during the 1980s. Machinery, equipment and vehicles, notably automobiles and spare parts, equipment for food, pulp-and-paper, mineral resource industry and agriculture as well as supplies of watercraft, aircraft, and of railway, power, and electrical equipment were the major German exports to the African countries. Concurrently, the German export of machine-building products dropped more than by a half in value terms in the 1980s. The complicated monetary and financial situation of many African countries has revealed itself primarily in an acute shortage of the means of payment, affecting negatively the interest of German companies to sell mechanical engineering products in the region.

The geographic distribution of trade with the African countries in the 1980s was mainly determined by traditional economic, cultural, and historical links, by the level of economic development of the continent's countries, their monetary and financial situation and solvency, by the degree of interest of the German industry in the supplies of raw materials and fuel from Africa, and by the opportunities for the German capital to penetrate into the economy of the African countries.

Germany's main trading partners in Africa are the SAR, Libya, Algeria, Egypt, Tunisia, Morocco, the Ivory Coast, Nigeria, Zimbabwe, and the Congo (Brazzaville). These 10 states account for 87.5% of Germany's import from the African continent. Germany is interested in expanding the geography of export-import transactions, including by way of developing the links with the African continent, as the majority of its countries are rich in natural resources.

The major obstacle on the way of increasing foreign trade expansion in this direction are the narrowness of the domestic market of the overwhelming majority of African countries, backwardness of their economy, the low level of industrial development, huge external debts, economic backwardness, and the population's low purchasing capacity. Despite an acute need for machines, machine-tools, vehicles, etc. they cannot yet absorb a significant part of the German export, 90% of which consists of manufactured goods. Furthermore, the German monopolies are forced to compete in the African market with both the former metropolitan countries – England and France, and the new suppliers – the US, Italy, and China.

The role of the so-called invisible articles has been steadily growing in the common structure of external economic links between Germany and the countries of Africa since the mid-1980s. These articles include those components of economic relations between countries, which do not mediate a turn-over of non-material assets. In terms of the GDP structure, these are the products of the non-material sphere of economy (except the proper capital flow, which is usually considered separately), trade in financial services, transport service, insurance, tourism, etc.

The leading role in the trade in financial services obviously belongs to the banks. Unlike most transnational banks (Tnbs) of the world, the German banks in Africa venture to extend their share holding in the local development banks, specialized investment banks of long-term crediting, and development corporations. Since the second half of the 1980s they have been gaining foot in the sphere of intermediate and long-term crediting and investment banking operations in the region. In particular, since the late 1980s the Federal Republic's TNBs (primarily through mediation as well as through direct share holding of the state corporations Deutsche Entwicklungsgesellschaft and KfW have been putting their investment capitals in the share capital of the major development banks in Lesotho, Mali, Morocco, Swaziland, and Somalia.

As to the insurance services, insurance of foreign trade is obviously the most significant segment of the African market for German companies, while the liability insurance (not related to the export-import transactions) is considerably less important. By virtue of poverty of the African population life and property insurance (except for freight insurance) are of little attraction to the German insurers.

Generally, in the overall structure of invisible trade the basis is formed by those branches, which attend primarily Germany's foreign trade with the countries of Africa. State insurance of foreign investments of the German companies, conclusion of intergovernmental agreements on protection of private investments, and tax privileges, among other things, function as components of this system. A special place in the system of investments protection in Africa and, in particular, in the SAR, is held by the state insurance company Hermes providing payment of indemnifications to private investors of capital from the federal budget in case of nationalization, changes in the country's policies, wars, introductions of restrictions on the transfer of profits, etc. Simultaneously the Hermes experts conduct marketing researches and determine the "attractiveness" of a certain country in terms of activity of the German private capital.

173

Tourism maintains strong independent positions among other "invisible" branches in the complex of German-African economic links. The tourist branch has been successfully developing for almost four decades, ever since the Germans "had discovered Africa" in the middle of the 1960s, despite all ascents and descents of the world conjuncture. The main flow of tourists from Germany, like decades ago, makes its way towards North Africa: Egypt, Tunisia, and Morocco. Tropical and Southern Africa, however, also have their due share of attention from the Germans. The income structure of the German companies clearly reflects the differentiation of the African countries. The abovementioned states of North Africa are largely oriented towards mass, small budget tourism (although at request the German consumer can also obtain expensive individual tours in the countries referred to). Tropical Africa overall offers more expensive tourist services for a more reduced number of people: individual "exotic" tours and safari for small groups. Tourism to exclusive de luxe resorts to the Seychelles, Mauritius, and Reunion increased in the 1990s.

The flow of African tourists to Germany is certainly less numerous. Nevertheless, it also tends to grow both due to the intensification of the European integration, to the establishment of the "Schengen border-control-free space" (hence a freer movement of Africans within Europe, in particular from the rather frequently visited former metropolitan countries to the neighboring states) and due to the formation in the African states of a rather numerous stratum of local well-to-do citizens inclined to travel.

The labor migration and to a lesser extent the movement of refugees still persist as the main form of movement of manpower from Africa to Germany. As to the quantitative scales of the African migration to Germany, one can assume that it will increase in the near future by virtue of a number of factors. These include primarily the ageing of the German population and a constant decline in the share of able-bodied citizens. On the other hand, the pauperization and destitution in many African states, aggravation of the unemployment problem largely related to the accelerated growth of population in many African countries as well as the aspiration to increase one's standard of living shall prompt the moving to Germany of huge masses of population from the less developed to the more developed countries, in particular, from a number of countries of Africa and the Arab East to Germany, the process forming an integral part of globalization.

In the 1990s the German capital still remained one of the large forces in Africa, although it ceded to some of its competitors. Nonetheless, a decrease of interest of the German companies to investing in Africa has come to light, bringing about an absolute reduction in the cost of direct German investments in Africa. Depression and unfavorable prospects for the production of export raw goods and the large external indebtedness of many African countries have affected adversely their economies, reducing their attractiveness to direct foreign investments. The slow, sometimes even negative rates of growth of the economy have led to a reduction in the profitability of the acting investments, diminishing thereby the stimuli to further investments. The restrictions on the transfer of profits in hard currency to the capital exporting country, imposed by the African countries, have also exerted a negative influence.

The prospects of activity of the German capital in the industry of African countries are directly related to the problem of investment profitability. A drop in the profitability of the German industrial investments in the manufacturing industry of African countries has induced many companies to start leaving Africa or to move their capitals to other regions of the world, for example, to Europe.

As to the small and medium-sized German business, its activity in the region has been hampered not only by the instability of the economic situation but also by a complicated, tangled, and – most of all – not meeting the modern free market demands, system of investment legislation in the majority of African states. Nevertheless, one should not consider that small and medium-sized German companies are completely disappointed in the opportunities to apply their capitals in the short-range outlook. The enduring interest is confirmed, in particular, by the constant search and application of new forms of activity in combination with the old, conventional ones. A number of circum-

175

stances of political, economic, and legal nature determine whether the process of disinvestment shall develop in future. A part of African governments is actively seeking to attract foreign investments, the investment codes have been liberalized in a number of countries; however, these stimuli have so far no serious effect on the inflow of the German capital in the African region.

The positions of the German banking capital were always strong in the African market; they have been affected to a lesser extent by the recession in the economies of African countries as against, for example, the positions of German companies. Two German banks, Deutsche Bank and Commerzbank, operate in Africa most actively. Both of them dispose of a wide branch and subsidiary network in Africa, both have operational experience in the region, going beyond several decades, the African operations are a traditional and rather appreciable part of these banks' activity. On the other hand, one cannot affirm that the aggravation of the economic climate has not in the least affected the activity of the German banking capital in Africa. The main difficulties hampering the expansion of the German banking in Africa are the constantly growing inflation and devaluation of the African national currencies.

This circumstance has induced the German banks to look for new forms (for example, forfeiting) and regions of activity. The German banks increasingly use the opportunities of cooperation with French banks, which enjoy a solid support on the part of the Communauté Financière Africaine, CFA (African Financial Community) in the African markets.

Unlike the private German capital in general (the major TNC excluded), the official capital has acted in the African markets rather successfully. This is exemplified by the activity of the German fund of development assistance. The fund is one of the largest investors in the African region. This was a consequence of a stable financial support of the state under a complete commercial and production independence of the Fund; regard for the recipient country's interests; a fruitful combination of the various business forms, such as investment practice, granting of loans as well as rendering various kinds of services; a careful selection of projects, their "double appraisal" in terms of the economic conditions of the country where they are to be implemented and in terms of viability of the project per se; flexible investment policies; and a comprehensive application of the co-investment practice in the implemented projects. However, with the emergence of such competitors for the African countries as the Central and Eastern European states, a change of priorities has began to take shape quite obviously. The Federal Republic began to pay more attention to its "zone of historical responsibility" and interests. Under the conditions of finiteness of the appropriated state resources this could only mean the dwindling of financing for the African programs.

As to the development of the social infrastructure, assistance there is provided mainly for the development of primary education, health services, and a family planning program.

In the second half of the 1990s, Africa ranked second by volumes and share of the ODA received from Germany, after the Asian region. The years 1996 and 1997 made an exception, when African states received more ODA from Germany than the Asian ones, the increase being predominantly on account of the North African region. Overall, the share of Africa in the German ODA varied during the period at issue between 31% and 37%, i.e. $^1/_3$ of the total Federal Republic's bilateral official development assistance was granted to the African states. The countries of Africa south of Sahara received from $^2/_3$ to $^3/_4$ of the German ODA.

In addition to financial aid, Germany pays considerable attention to technical assistance to the developing countries of Africa: Germany is distinguished by a high share of such assistance in the total amount of aid (approximately 30%) in comparison to other donor countries. Technical assistance supplements financial aid and creates the conditions for a more efficient implementation of the project and program aid and of private investments. In the authors' opinion, the paramount attention to the training of the national staff under the program of German technical support means a real assistance to the development of African countries. This form of aid influences directly the creation of a management link capable to work efficiently under the open mar-

177

ket economy conditions. On the other hand, this direction of aid simultaneously serves the German commercial interests, for in the course of technical cooperation useful personal contacts are established, a more comprehensive familiarization with the system of values of the German way of life, with the main principles of German organization of economy, business development, and with the use of modern technologies occurs. Consequently, a favorable milieu is being created, in which the German companies can compete henceforth more successfully under market conditions.

Although ODA's main goal is combating poverty, destitution, famine, illiteracy, and illnesses, the donor countries, including Germany, also derive economic benefits from it. The ODA is being spent, for example, on remunerating German experts in the developing countries, including the African ones, while the goods from the donor-country are accorded priority in the local national markets. The ODA plays a part of a "door opener" for the export of the German production and promotion of the German capitals in the African markets.

The official development assistance granted by the OECD member nations to the African states can by no means be referred to pure charity. The industrial powers, including Germany, by manipulating with the distribution, structure, and volumes of aid create the necessary conditions for promoting their goods, capitals, and services in the African markets. Providing assistance permits the developed states to impose certain political demands, conditioning the granting of aid on the "agreeable" or "disagreeable" nature of the political regime in this or that country. In other words, granting ODA in the epoch of globalization in many respects serves as the precondition for promoting transnational corporations and banks in the new markets of the developing states and involving the latter in the modern system of international labour division, advancing thereby the interests of a limited circle of world economy subjects.

Recapitulating his research, the authors consider important to highlight that the decrease of German interest to the African region is a form of manifestation of complex processes, whose essence is not exhausted by a simple reduction in the cost volumes of economic links. The system of German-African economic relations per se is changing in quality terms.

Firstly, the "external" decline of interest to Africa has occurred against the background of the German capital reserving overall its firm positions in the African economy. Secondly, the reduction in the volumes of trade and capital export in the second half of the 1990s was accompanied by an increase in the German aid to Africa on multilateral basis, primarily within the EU. Thirdly, the decrease in Germany's concernment in the import of certain commodities from the African region has not led to an essential reduction of the German business in the relevant spheres. Fourthly, the small and medium-sized German business has maintained its potential interest in working on the African continent. Nevertheless, the reduction of the necessary state support from the German party as well as an adverse investment climate in many African countries were the main obstacles for a large-scale entry of small and medium-sized German companies in the African market.

As the world's economic woes deepened in 2008-2009, Africa's leaders are delivering a strong message that the international community must help the continent protect the development gains of recent years. Mineral and oil exporters have been hit particularly hard. Copper prices went down over 60 per cent. Oil, at around $45 a barrel, was at a fraction of its highs of over $140 less than a year ago. Prices for rubber, cotton, palm oil and timber also went well down. Shrinking world demand translated into mounting unemployment. The mining sector was particularly badly affected, but food production also dived. For hundreds of thousands if not millions of Africans the threat of persistent hunger and starvation loomed again.

In a report prepared for the 2 April 2009 meeting of the Group of 20 (G-20), a high-level consultative body, at which South Africa is the continent's only representative, a committee of 10 African finance ministers and central bank governors set up to monitor the crisis, has told world leaders that they must honour their commitments to increase aid, improve trade access and agree to a fairer, more flexible way of managing international financial affairs[1].

Germany continues to play an important role in those efforts. In a recent manifestation of its solidarity and support to all-Africa causes, the German government has agreed in April 2009 to finance the construction of the new building for the Peace and Security Department of the African Union (AU) estimated to cost about 20 Million Euro. The new building will be centrally located on the grounds of the AU in Addis Ababa, adjacent to the AU's new Conference Center.

In an open and transparent architectural competition in Berlin, 17 architects were invited to design the new building. The architectural designs for the new building will now be exhibited at the Africa Union Commission (AUC) Headquarters, in Addis Ababa, Ethiopia.

The modern and representative Peace and Security Building will be environmentally friendly and energy efficient. It will comprise approximately 11.500 m² gross floor area (GFA) and offer approximately 370 new jobs. GTZ was commissioned by the German Federal Foreign Office for the development and execution of the AU Peace and Security project.

On the whole, the German capital has managed to reserve its firm positions in the African countries in such important spheres as production and processing of some minerals, chemical industry and metallurgy, industrial assembly of products from the German semi-finished goods and parts, wholesale and retail trade, light and food industry, banking and insurance business, tourism and hotels, etc. Combined with foreign trade, certain cultural, historical, and personal links (especially in the south of Africa), the impact of the EU standards on education, administrative and judicial system, Germany's influence on the independent countries of Africa remains significant and will hardly decrease in the foreseeable future.

---

[1] Aftica Renewal. V. 23, No. 1, April 2009. P. 13.

BIBLIOGRAPHY

Official publications and statistics

1. Africa Contemporary Record 1997–1998. Ed. by C. Legum. L.
2. African Development Indicators 2002. The World Bank. Washington, 2002.
3. Africa Research-Bulletin. L.
4. Balance of Payment Manual, International Monetary Fund, 5th edition, Washington DC, 1993.
5. Bericht der Komission für die Reform des Auswärtigen Dienstes. Bonn, 2001.
6. BIS Quarterly Review, International banking and financial market developments Bank for International, Basel, 1990–2001.
7. Bulletin des Presse- und Informationsamtes der Bundesregierung. Bonn.
8. Debt stocks, debt flows and the balance of payments, Bank for International Settlements, International Monetary Fund, Organisation for Economic Co-operation and Development, World Bank P., 1994.
9. Development Co-operation, Organisation for Economic Co-operation and Development, Paris, 1990–2000.
10. Deutscher Bundestag. Stenographischer Bericht 5U, Sitzung, 1997. Bd 103, Bonn, 1997.
11. Dritter Bericht zur Entwicklungspolitik der Bundesregierung. Bonn. November 1997. Anlage 11.
12. Entwicklungspolitik. Fünfter Jahresbericht. Bonn, 1993.
13. Entwicklungspolitik. Jahresbericht. Bonn, 2001, 2002.
14. Entwicklungspolitik. Materialien. Bonn.
15. Exportmärkte Deutschlands. Profile und Statistiken zu den 50 wichtigsten Abnehmerländern deutscher Produkte. Köln. 2002.
16. Foreign Direct Investment in Africa: Performance and Potential. UNITED NATIONS, New York and Geneva, 1999.
17. Global Development Finance (до 1996 World Debt Tables). The World Bank, 1990–2000.
18. Global Development Finance. 1997, v. 1–2. World Bank. Washington DC, 1997.
19. Handbuch der empirischen Sozialforschungen. Stuttgart, 1996, Bd 5.
20. Handbuch der Entwicklungshilfe, II A 60, BR. Nomos–Verlag. Bonn–Bad Godeeberg.
21. Human Development Report 1996, United Nations Development Programme. NY, 1999, Overview.
22. International Financial Statistics. Washington DC, 1990–2001.

23. Journalisten Handbuch. Entwicklungspolitik. Hrsg., Bonn, 1997–2002.

24. North–South: A Programm for Survival. The Report of the Independent Comission on International Development Issues under the Chairmanship of W. Brandt. L., 2000.

25. Orientierungsrahmen 85. Text und Diskussion. Hrsg. Oertzen P., Emke H. Bonn–Bad Godesberg, 1996.

26. Partners in Development. Report of the Comission on International Development. N.Y. – L., 2000.

27. Perspectives in Afro-German Relations. Reports and Discussions. Bonn, 1995.

28. Staff Study of the Crime and Secrecy: The Use of Offshore Banks and Companies, Washington. DCUS Congress February 1983.

29. Statistisches Jahrbuch für die Bundesrepublik Deutschland. Wiesbaden. 1991–2002.

30. Survey of Economic Conditions in Africa, UNECA, .Addis Ababa. 1990–2001.

31. The Market, Democracy and Development in Africa. A Keynote Address at the 40th Anniversary of Africa Confidential by K.Y. Amoako UN Under-Secretary-General and Executive Secretary of ECA, 19 April, 2000, London.

32. Transforming African Economies, UNECA. Addis Ababa, 2001.

33. Trends in Developing Economies. The World Bank, 1995–2000.

34. World Development Report. The World Bank. Washington DC 1980–2000.

35. World Economic Outlook. International Monetary Fund. UN, Washington DC, 1995–2000.

Monographs and articles

36. *Баскин В.С.* Капиталистическая "помощь" развивающимся странам – механизм, характер и направление воздействия на страны Африки. М., Наука, 1982.

37. *Бессонов С.А.,* Проблемы государственного планирования в странах Африки. М., Наука, 1987.

38. *Былиняк С.А.* Развивающиеся страны: мирохозяйственные проблемы во взаимозависимом мире. М., 1990.

39. *Гевелинг Л.В.* Феномен и механизмы деструктивного развития обществ переходного типа. Восток. М., 2000, № 5, с. 76–92.

40. *Голанский М.М.* Новые тенденции в мировой экономике и участь отставших стран. М., 1995.

41. *Голанский М.М.* Современная политэкономия. Что век грядущий нам готовит? Эдиториал УРСС, М., 1998, с. 99.

42. *Динкевич А.И.* Транснациональные монополии и развивающиеся страны // МКХ – транснациональный капитал и развивающиеся страны. М., 1988, с. 23–73.

43. Зарубежные концепции экономического развития стран Африки. критический анализ. М., 1980.

44. *Кузнецов В.С.* Международный валютный фонд: новая роль в мирохозяйственных связях. М., 1999.

45. *Лушин, С.И.* Финансовая глобализация // Финансы, 2001, № 3, с. 60–62.

46. Мировая экономика: нарастающий процесс глобализации (Прогноз на 2000–2015 годы). ИМЭМО РАН, М., 1998.

47. *Михайлов Д.* Мировая экономика тенденции 90-х годов. Наука. М., 1999.

48. *Норт Д.* Институты, институциональные изменения и функционирование экономики. М., 1997.

49. *Обминский Э.Е.* Глобальные интересы и национальный эгоизм. Экономический аспект. М.: Международные отношения, 1990.

50. *Осипов Ю.М.* Либерализация валютной политики // Африка: новые тенденции в экономической политике. ИВЛ. М., 2000, с. 115–132.

51. *Павлов В.В.* Политика транснациональных банков в Африке. (Проблемы и тенденции 80–90-х годов). М., 2000.

52. Развивающиеся страны: в сетях финансовой зависимости / Под ред. Г.П. Солюса. Финансы и статистика. М., 1990.

53. Расколотая и погрязшая в долгах // Азия и Африка сегодня, 1996, М., № 1, январь, с. 34–36.

54. *Рощин Г.Э.* ТНК и перспектива развития стран Африки. Наука. М., 1992.

55. *Рунов Б.Б.* Интеграция Африки в глобальную экономику: Тенденции, проблемы, перспективы. "XXI век – Согласие". М., 1999.

56. *Симония Н.А.* Глобализация и неравномерность мирового развития // Мировая экономика и международные отношения, 2001, № 3, с. 37.

57. *Солодовников В.Г.* Вывоз капитала. Наука. М., 1957.

58. Финансовая глобализация и ее последствия для финансовой системы развивающихся и "переходных" государств // Финансовый бизнес, 2000, № 1, с. 14–20.

59. *Фитуни Л.Л.* Финансовая глобализация и бегство капитала из России // Россия в окружающем мире: 2000. Изд-во МНЭПУ. М., 2000, с. 97–111.

60. *Фридман Л.А.* Современный экономический рост. Вестник Московского Университета. Серия "Востоковедение". М., 1988. № 1. С. 3–19.

61. *Хорос В.* Глобализация и периферия. Мировая экономика и Международные отношения, М., 1999, № 12, с. 111–118.

62. *Цимайло А.В.* Платежный баланс и валютный курс (в теории и практике ведущих стран Запада). Институт Европы АН СССР. М., Наука, 1991.

63. *Эльянов А.Я.* Перспективы и проблемы развивающихся стран (прогноз на 2000–2015) М., 1999.

64. *Яшкин В.А.,* Экономика развивающихся стран на рубеже 90-х гг. и перспективы ее развития // Развивающиеся страны в социально-экономических структурах современного мира. М., Наука, 1991, с. 117–178.

65. *Adam Markus C.* and *Victor Ginsburgh.* The effects of irregular markets on macroeconomic policy: Some estimates for Belgium // European Economic Review, 1985, 29/1, pp. 15–33.

66. Afrika und Bonn. Hrsg. Bley H., Tetzlaff R. Hamburg, 1998.

67. Afrika zwischen Tradition und Fortschritt. Hrsg. Ortlieb H.-D. und Zwernemann J. Hamburg, 2000.

68. Agrarreform in der Dritten Welt. Hrsg. Eisenhans H. Frankfurt/M.–New York, 1999.

69. *Assel H.G.* Demokratischer Sozialpluralismus. München–Wien. 1995.

70. *Behrendt R.F.* Soziale Strategie für Entwicklungsländer. Entwurf einer Entwicklungssoziologie. Frankfurt/M., 1988.

71. *Bergmann H.* Modernisierung durch Genossenschaften. München, 1982.

72. *Behtold H.* Staaten ohne Nation. Sozialismus als Machtfaktor in Asien und Afrika. Stuttgart, 1980.

73. *Blumental C.* Die Deutschen Exportmaerkte im Ueberblick. Berlin, 2002.

74. *Bodemer K.* Entwicklungshilfepolitik für wen? München, 1994.

75. *Böll W., Matke O.* Das Eigenpotential im Entwicklungsprozess. B. (W.), 1992.

76. *Breyer K.* Moskaus Faust in Afrika. Stuttgart, 1989.

77. *Buhl W.* Transnationale Politik. Stuttgart, 1998.

78. *Clapham R.* Marktwirtschaft in Entwicklungsländern. Freiburg, 1993.

79. *Czempiel E.-O.* Friedenspolitik im Südlichen Afrika. Eine Strategie für die Budesrepublik Deutschland. München, 1996.

80. *Czempiel E.-O.* Hrsg. Die anachronistische Souveränität. Köln, 1989.

81. Das Nord–Süd Problem. Konflikte zwischen Industrie- und Entwicklungsländern. Hrsg. Bohnet M., München, 1981.

82. Der Konflikt in Südafrika. Expertengespräche in Bonn 29–30 Mai 1990. Hrsg. F.-E. Stiftung. Bonn, 1990.

83. Die christliche Konzeption der pluralistischen Demokratie. Stuttgart, 1987.

84. Die Krise in der Soziologie. Kritische Studien zum 37. Deutschen Soziologentag in der BRD. Hrsg. Krysmansky H. B., 1995.

85. *Eisermann G.* Hrsg. Die Krise der Soziologie. Stuttgart, 1990.

86. Entwicklungsprobleme – interdisziplinär. Hrsg. Peter H., Hauser J. Bern–Stuttgart, 1976.

87. Entwicklungsmodell Tansania. Hrsg. Pfennig W., Voll K, Weber H. Frankfurt/M., 1990.

88. *Eppler E.* Wenig Zeit für die Dritte Welt. Stuttgart–Berlin, 1992;

89. *Eppler E.* Ende oder Wende? Von der Nachbarkeit des Notwendigen. Stuttgart, 1986.

90. *Eppler E.* Das Schwerste ist Glaubwürdigkeit. Hamburg, 1988.

91. *Faber R.* Abendland. Ein politischer Kampfbegriff. Hildesheim, 1989.

92. *Fischer S.* Wirtschaftliche Eckdaten im internationalen Vergleich. Koeln, 1999.

93. *Friederich R.* Das grosse Buch der Dritten Welt. Schlüssel zum Verstehen der Weltprobleme. Enseling und Laiblin Verlag, 1988.

94. *Friedländer P., Liebscher G.* Neokolonialismus in der Krise. B., 1988.

95. *Fritsch B.* Die vierte Welt. Stuttgart, 2000.

96. *Genscher H.-D.* Aussenpolitik im Dienste von Sicherheit und Freiheit: Stuttgart, 1996.

97. *Gerth-Wellmann H. und Kayser D.* Die industrielle Zusammenarbeit zwischen EG und den AKP–Staaten im Rahmen der Lome–Politik. München, London, 1990.

98. *Goetze D.* Entwicklingssoziologie. München, 1996.

99. *Grimm K.* Theorien der Unterentwicklung und Entwicklungsstrategien. Öpladen, 1979.

100. *Guth W.* Entwicklungspolitik in der Krise. Tübingen, 1992.

101. *Hardach G.* Deutschland in der Weltwirtschaft 1985–1995. Frankfurt/M., 1997.

102. *Harding L.* Afrikanische Politik in Südlichem Afrika. München, 1995.

103. *Havemann H.A.* Die Konzeption einer Zentralstelle für Entwicklungstechnikmodelle–Aufgaben–Organisation–Verwirklichung. Aachen, 1993.

104. *Heintz P.* Die Zukunft der Entwicklung. Stuttgart–Wien, 1994.

105. *Hemmer H.-R.* Wirtschaftsprobleme der Entwicklungsländer. München, 1997.

106. *Hesse K. Ischinger W.* Die Entwicklungsschwelle. Bonn, 1993.

107. "Hilfswissenschaft für die Dritte Welt oder "Wissenschaftsimperialismus"? Hrsg. K-M. Khan, N. V. Matthies. München, 1996.

108. *Hofmeier R., Schattner S.* u.a. Die wirtschaftliche und rohstohffliche Bedeutung Afrikas und seiner einzelner Regionen (Südafrica, Schwarzafrika, Nordafrika) für die Bundesrepublik Deutschland. Hamburg, 2001.

109. *Hopfenbeck W.* Planung und Errichtung von kompletten Indstrieanlagen in Entwicklungsländern. München, 1994.

110. Investitionen statt Klassenkampf. Hrsg. Frickhöffer W. u. a. Bonn, Internationale Politik. Wiesbaden, 1990.

111. Internationale Wirtschaftsordnung. Hrsg. Gröner H. und Schüller A. Stuttgart-nNew York, 1998.

112. *Kaiser K.* Transnationale Politik in: Die anachronistische Souveränität. Hrsg. Czempiel Ö. Köln, 1999.

113. *Kirchgässner Gebhard.* Verfahren zur Erfassung des in der Schattenwirtschaft erarbeiteten Sozialprodukts // Allgemeines Statistisches Archiv, 1994, 68/4, pp. 378–405.

114. *Kunhardt A.* Deutsche Exporte nach Afrika. Hamburg, 1998.

115. *Mandel E., Wolf W.* Ende der Krise oder die Krise ohne Ende? Wiesbaden, 1997.

116. *Maier M.* Stärken und Schwächen der Afrikanischen Wirtschaft. Bonn, 1998.

117. *Marloh D.* Deutsche Direktinvestitionen im Ausland. Hamburg, 2000.

118. *Meier H.* Die geplante Misere. Zur soziologischen Problematik fehlgeschlagener Entwicklungsprojekte. 1991.

119. *Meyers R.* Die Lehre von internationalen Beziehungen. Düsseldorf, 1997.

120. *Michel H., Ochel W.* Ländliche Industrialisierung in Entwicklungsländern. München, 1987.

121. *Morgan R.* West Germany's Policy Agenda. Wash., 1988.

122. *Narten D.* Die Bevölkerungsstruktur in ihrer Bedeutung für das wirtschaftliche Wachstum der Entwicklungsländer. München, 1990.

123. Nationalismus. Hrsg. Winkler H. A. Königstein, 1978.

124. Nationalismus und sozialer Wandel. Hrsg. Dann O. Hamburg, 1978.

125. *Offergeld R.* Entwicklungshilfe. Abenteuer oder Politik? Stuttgart, 1980.

126. *Orlieb H.-D.* Was wird aus Afrika? Zürich, 1997.

127. *Pätzoldt B.* Ausländerstudium in der BRD. Köln, 2002.

128. *Pfeffer K.-H.* Die Entwicklungsländer in soziologischer Sicht. Hamburg, 1997.

129. *Philipp K.* Probleme der technischen Zusammenarbeit mit den am wenigsten entwickelten Ländern. Tübingen, 1989.

130. *Plank U., Ziehe J.* Land und Agrarsoziologie. Stuttgart,1979.

131. Polarität und Interdependenz. Beiträge zu Fragen der Internationalen Politik. Baden-Baden, 1978.

132. Probleme internationaler Organisationen und Behörden bei Katastropheneinsätze in Entwicklungsländern, Köln, 1994.

133. Probleme des Dritten Weges. Hrsg. Mansilla H. Darmstadt, 1984.

134. *Remmele W.* Die Selbstdarstellung der BRD im Ausland durch den Rundfunk als Problem des Staats- und Völkerrechts. Frankfurt/M., 2001.

135. Rechtfertigung der Elite. Hrsg. Kaltenbrunner G.-K. München, 2002.

136. *Rennert V.* Die wichtigsten deutschen Unternehmen in Afrika. Tübingen, 1999.

137. *Riegel K.-G.* Politische Soziologie unterindustrialisierter Gesellschaften: Entwicklungsländer. Wiesbaden, 1996.

138. *Rohe R.* Die Südafrikapolitik der Bundesrepublik Deutschland. München, 1996

139. *Schütte H. G.,* Ortlieb H.-D. Afrika betet anders. Hamburg, 1998.

140. *Senft J.* Entwicklungshilfe oder Entwicklungspolitik. Münster, 1988.

141. *Senghaas D.* Hrsg. Peripherer Kapitalismus. Analysen über Abhängigkeit und Unterentwicklung. Frankfurt/M., 1994.

142. *Senghaas D.* Weltwirtschaftsordnung und Entwicklungspolitik– Plädoeyer für eine Dissoziation. Frankfurt/M., 1998.

143. *Sieberg H.* Dritte Welt–Vierte Welt. Hildesheim–New York, 1977.

144. Soziale Marktwirtschaft als nationale und internationale Ordnung. Bonn, 2001.

145. *Splell O.* Die Politik des Kulturaustausches. München, 1997.

146. *Streeton P.* Aid to Africa. A Policy Outline for the 1990's. N. Y.– L., 1999.

147. *Tetzlaff R.* Die Weltbank: Machtinstrument der USA oder Hilfe für die Entwicklungsländer. München–London, 1990.

148. *Tetzlaff R* Wirtschaftliche Globalisierung und Demokratisierung – ein Widerspruch? In: Globalisierung: Chancen und Herausforderungen für die Entwicklungszusammenarbeit, hrsg. von der GTZ in Zusammenarbeit mit dem BMZ, Eschborn 1998.

149. *Tetzlaff R* Afrika zwischen Demokratisierung und Staatszerfall, in: Aus Politik und Zeitgeschichte. Beilage zum „Parlament", B 21/98 (15 Mai 1998), S. 3–15.

150. *Tetzlaff R* Was wird aus der Dritten Welt?, in: Marion Gräfin Dönhoff und Theo Sommer (Hrsg.), Was steht uns bevor? Mutmaßungen über das 21. Jahrhundert. Aus Anlaß des 80. Geburtstages von Helmut Schmidt, Berlin (Siedler) 1999.

151. *Todenhöfer J.-G.* Wachstum für alle. Plädoyer für eine internationale soziale Marktwirtschaft. Stuttgart, 1986.

152. Unterentwicklung. Bd 2. Hrsg. von Tibi B., Brandes V. Frankfurt/M., 1985.

153. *Veit W.* Nationale Emanzipation. Entwicklungsstrategie und Aussenpolitik im Tropischen–Afrika. Die Beispiele Elfenbeinküste und Guinea. München, 1988.

154. *Vester F.* Denken, Lernen, Vergessen. Stuttgart, 1995.

155. *Vieregge H.* Parteistiftungen. Baden-Baden, 1987.

156. *Wander H.* Bevölkerungswachstum und Konsumstruktur in Entwicklungsländern. Tübingen, 1997.

157. *Weck Hannelore.* Schattenwirtschaft: Eine Möglichkeit zur Einschränkung der öffentlichen Verwaltung? Eine ökonomische Analyse. Bern-Frankfurt 1983.

158. *Widmaier U.* Politische Gestaltungen als Problem der Organisation von Interessen. Königstein, 1988.

159. *Wischnewsky H.-J.* Entwicklungsshilfe und Wissenschaft. Giessen, 1988.

160. *Welt, Leo G.B.* Blocked funds: aspects of capital flight, L., Euromoney Books, 1990, 129 p.

161. *Werner Christian.* Die Beschäftigungswirkungen der Schattenwirtschaft. Pfaffenweiler, Centaurus 1990.

Periodicals

162. Азия и Африка сегодня. М.

163. Банковский Бюллетень (ЦБР). Москва, 1995–1996.

164. Бюллетень иностранной коммерческой информации (БИКИ). М.

165. Ведомости. М.

166. Вопросы экономики. М.

167. Восток (до 1990 – Народы Азии и Африки). М.

168. Деньги и кредит. М.

169. Известия. М.

170. Мировая экономика и международные отношения (МЭМО). М.

171. Сегодня. М.

172. Финансы. М.

173. Экономика и жизнь, М.
174. Africa. L.
175. Afrika–heute. Bonn.
176. Afrika–Spectrum. Hamburg.
177. Afrique–Asie. P.
178. Argument. Frankfurt/MT
179. Aus Politik und Zeitgeschichte. Beilage zum Das Parlament , Bonn
180. Auslandskurier. Bonn.
181. Aussenpolitik. Bonn.
182. Blätter für die deutsche und internationale Politik. Köln.
183. Blick durch-die Wirtschaft. Frankfurt/M.
184. Capital. Hamburg.
185. Daily Times. Lagos.
186. Deutsche Aussenpolitik. B.
187. Deutsche Volkszeitung. Düsseldorf.
188. Development Finance. Washington, DC.
189. Dokumentation der Zeit. B.
190. Dritte Welt Magazin. Köln.
191. Dritte Welt. Mainz.
192. Economist. L.
193. Entwicklung und Zusammenarbeit. Bonn.
194. Entwicklungspolitik. Spiegel der Presse. BMZ. Bonn.
195. Europa–Archiv. Bonn.
196. Financial Crime Review. L.
197. Frankfurter Allgemeine Zeitung. Frankfurt/M.
198. Frankfurter Rundschau. Frankfurt/M.
199. Handelsblatt. Düsseldorf.
200. Horizont. B.
201. IMF Survey, IMF. Washington DC
202. Intereconomics. Hamburg.
203. International Herald Tribüne. P.
204. Internationales Afrika–Forum. München.
205. Internationales Asien–Forum. Hamburg.
206. IPW–Berichte. B.
207. Journal of Financial Crime. L.
208. Journal of Money Laundering Control. L.
209. Kölner Zeitschrift für Soziologie und Sozialpsychologie. Köln.
210. Liberal. Bonn
211. Management. Wiesbaden.
212. Merkur. Stuttgart.
213. Mitarbeit. Köln.
214. Moderne Welt. Düsseldorf.

215. Neue Gesellschaft. Bonn.
216. Neues Deutschland . Berlin.
217. New York Times. N.Y.
218. Parlament. Bonn.
219. Politische Studien. München.
220. Spiegel. Hamburg.
221. Stern. Hamburg.
222. The Financial Times. L.
223. The Journal of International Banking Regulation. L.
224. Übersee Rundschau. Hamburg.
225. Universitas. Stuttgart.
226. Vierteljahresberichte. Bonn.
227. Vorwärts. Bonn–Bad Godesberg.
228. Wahrheit. B. (W).
229. Welt. Hamburg.
230. Weltwirtschaft. Kiel.
231. West Africa. L.
232. Wirtschaftsdienst. Hamburg.
233. Wirtschaftswoche. Frankfurt/M.
234. World Development. L.
235. Zeit. Hamburg.
236. Zeitschrift für ausländische Landwirtschaft. Frankfurt/M.
237. Zeitschrift für den Kulturaustausch. Tübingen.
238. Zeitschrift für Politik. München.

The Internet

239. www.imf.org
240. www.worldbank.org
241. www.oecd.org
242. www.bmz.de
243. www.gtz.org
244. www.safri.com
245. www.africa-business.com
246. www.ahk.com
247. www.german-embassy.org
248. www.ahkmena.com
249. www.germanchamber.co.za
250. www.resbank.co.za
251. www.satour.de
252. www.boc.gov.tn
253. www.auslaender.de

254. www.ilo.org
255. www.unctad.org
256. www.rrz.uni-hamburg.de
257. www.gtai.de
258. www.bundesregierung.de
259. www.destatis.de
260. www.thedatareport.org
261. www.euroresources.org
262. www.aicgs.org

Научное издание

**Irina Abramova, Curt Stoll,
Konstantin Tkachenko**

**GERMANY IN AFRICA: RECONCILING
BUSINESS AND DEVELOPMENT**

*Утверждено к печати
Институтом Африки РАН*

Зав. РИО *Н.А. Ксенофонтова*
Компьютерная верстка и дизайн
Г.М. Абишевой

*При создании коллажа обложки использованы элементы фотографии Gujer
"Mujer Mursi #4", представленной по свободной лицензии Creative Commons.*

This is a reprint of the original Moscow 2009 edition by
MEABOOKS Inc.
34 CH. DU BOISE
LAC-BEAUPORT
QC G3B 2A5
CANADA

WWW.MEABOOKS.COM

Printed in the United States
By Bookmasters